Women Survivors
of Childhood Sexual Abuse
Healing Through Group Work

Beyond Survival

HAWORTH Marriage & the Family
Terry S. Trepper, PhD
Senior Editor

Women Survivors
of Childhood Sexual Abuse
Healing Through Group Work

Beyond Survival

Judy Chew, PhD

The Haworth Press
New York • London

The Haworth Press, Inc., 10 Alice Street, Binghamton, NY 13904-1580

Cover design by Marylouise E. Doyle.

Library of Congress Cataloging-in-Publication Data

Chew, Judy.
  Women survivors of childhood sexual abuse : healing through group work : beyond survival / Judy Chew.
    p.   cm.
  Includes bibliographical references and index.
  ISBN 0-7890-0284-1 (alk. paper).
  1. Adult child sexual abuse victims—Rehabilitation. 2. Group psychotherapy. I. Title.
RC569.5.A28C47 1997
616.85′83690651—dc21

                                                                            97-7517
                                                                               CIP

To my mother, Mei Hing Lee,
and to the memory of my father, Ging Gar Chew.
Their lives of industriousness, hard work, challenge,
and reward have taught me
about the capacity and resiliency of the human spirit.

and

To John,
for the many blessings.

ABOUT THE AUTHOR

Judy Chew, PhD, is a chartered psychologist, Training Coordinator at the University of Calgary's Counselling Services, and Adjunct Assistant Professor in the Department of Educational Psychology at the University of Calgary in Alberta, Canada. Dr. Chew maintains a small private practice and is a clinical member of the American Association for Marriage and Family Therapy. Her professional experience and interests include training/supervision; women's issues; family of origin work; the resolving of physical, emotional, and sexual abuse; relationship counseling; and the promotion of individual choices that enhance emotional, physical, spiritual, and social well-being.

CONTENTS

Foreword

Experiencing my daughter Zoe grow into a person has been the most extraordinary blessing of my life. Among other things, it seems a microcosm for the contradictions and delicate balance of all aspects of life. She is alternatingly—and often simultaneously!—vulnerable and strong, independent and dependent, confident and uncertain, distinct yet universal. Her wisdom seems beyond her years, but her knowledge and skill base develops only as a result of attentiveness and time. The seeds of her beauty and strength require much water, shade, and warmth. We are often reminded of the African proverb that it takes an entire village to raise a child.

In this process of growth and development, tragedy and loss cannot be avoided. People die, traumas strike, trusts are betrayed, and suffering is experienced. No matter how safe we try to make life, no one escapes its pains and unfairnesses. Of course, what we can and must do is provide a space in which such experiences can be acknowledged, processed, and integrated.

In this regard, childhood sexual abuse can be seen as damaging on three levels. First, it is a horrible experience or set of experiences that should not have happened, but did. The community is responsible for protecting each of its members from violation, and it fails in the case of sexual abuse. Second, an act of sexual abuse carves a curse into the vulnerable organic weave of the victim's mind, body, and soul. The ideas of "you're worthless," "you deserve this," "your body should be violated" are emblazoned into the core identity of the person, forming the basis for self-denigrating thoughts, feelings, and behaviors. And third, attempts to communicate (and hence, integrate) the trauma are often blocked with denial, threat, minimization, or more abuse. In short, the experience of the trauma stays locked in the person's neuromuscular consciousness, unable to move from a present experience to a complete memory.

Thus, when we encounter adults struggling with memories of childhood sexual abuse, we see traumatic experiences and events still trying to complete themselves. The experiences are not in the past; they are still in the present reality of the person. When active, they are accompanied by "breaks" in senses of beingness, belongingness, and relatedness. Without such connections, life is an unbearably lonely and frightening experience.

From this perspective, our task as healers and therapists is to provide some opportunities for the relational connections to be reestablished, both to acknowledge and deal with what happened, as well as to open attention to the possibilities of life beyond the trauma. There are a number of writers who have addressed how this might be done in individual therapy—some of the best include Dolan, Herman, van der Kolk, and Briere—but very few who have offered ideas about how group work might be helpful in this regard.

This book by Judy Chew is therefore a very timely and important contribution to the field. Dr. Chew writes in an exceptionally lucid and helpful way, describing the means and rationale for a group therapy. One of her strongest emphases is that a person is more than just an "abuse survivor"; in fact, other identities may be more developed and more important. Thus good therapy respects and connects with the nonabused parts of the person as well as with traumatized parts. While reading this book, I was reminded of an anecdote told by Ram Dass. He was sitting around with a good friend and a rabbi, and the rabbi asked Ram Dass how his Jewish upbringing influenced his present spiritual identity. The somewhat impish friend replied, "You have to remember that Ram Dass is only Jewish on his parents' side!" Similarly, Judy Chew always seems to keep in mind that her clients may have been abused in one area of their lives, but there are always other sides that are crucial to living "beyond survival."

To move beyond survival, one must usually find ways to first move through it. Dr. Chew presents some excellent methods and ideas for how we may help people do just that. I am very happy to see this impressive book be published. I hope you find it as valuable as I did.

Stephen Gilligan, PhD
Encinitas, CA

Preface

PURPOSE OF THE TEXT

Researchers and clinicians alike are commended for their concerted efforts in articulating and expanding the body of knowledge pertaining to childhood sexual abuse. However, very little of the existing literature actually provides the "how-to's" of conducting a group of this nature *along with* the theoretical and philosophical bases of the steps involved.

In exploring the literature, theoretical, anecdotal (case studies), evaluative, philosophical, or self-help approaches are outlined. While these contributions provide a necessary foundation for research and clinical practice, there is a crucial need for information that is directly applicable for clinical practice in group work. In other words, it is necessary to bridge theory with practice in a systematic and practical way. This task is accomplished by acknowledging the vital contributions made by those who are "in the know" and who possess wisdom with respect to personal experience, clinical practice, research, and theoretical knowledge in the area of childhood sexual abuse.

This text will offer a number of benefits:

1. to lessen the separateness between theoreticians and practitioners;
2. to bring together counselors/practitioners in their professional efforts to address sexual abuse;
3. to provide counselors with creative opportunities to promote client initiatives and participation in the larger community (e.g., academic, social, vocational, political, and spiritual); and
4. to provide ideas and suggestions for other professionals who are considering a group program or exploring new ideas for group work.

USING THIS BOOK: AN OVERVIEW

This book serves as a guideline for counselors working with individuals who have experienced sexual abuse. Of critical importance for facilitators are: adequate training in addressing sexual abuse issues in a counseling context, experience working with groups, and competent clinical skills. Furthermore, consideration needs to be given to the specific needs of each group, personal characteristics of the individuals, the interests of the participants, and the resources at hand. For example, more time might be allocated to mastery themes if the group has six members as opposed to eight. Instead of a four-week long group where two participants tell their story each week, groups might only be three weeks long involving the storytelling of two individuals each week. Or, to accommodate the needs of students at certain times of the academic year, the group might be shortened or lengthened accordingly.

A session-by-session account is outlined in the following chapters. Facilitators are encouraged and invited to use their own resourcefulness, creativity, and clinical skills to shape the sessions in ways that best meet the needs of the group.

Acknowledgments

This text was made possible by the courageous and honest voices of the individuals who shared their stories of pain and victimization, and their pathways to survival, hope, and beyond survival. Without the wisdom and generous contribution of these women, our theories and practices would be irrelevant misrepresentations of the experiences of many. Above all, this text is a tribute to those individuals who have allowed their untold stories to be told, and to those individuals who will embark on the healing journey.

The experience of writing a book involves tenacity, enthusiasm, dedication, clarity of thought, and the combined efforts of others. Such efforts are essential for the translation of ideas and thoughts into a completed work. In particular, I am grateful to the wonderful staff at The Haworth Press for making this endeavor exciting and rewarding for me: Terry S. Trepper, PhD, Bill Palmer, Patricia M. Brown, Peg Marr, Dawn M. Krisko, Susan Trzeciak Gibson, Deb Johnston, Donna Biesecker, Tom Rushmer, Marylouise Doyle, and Sandra Jones Sickels.

I extend my gratitude to Stephen Gilligan, PhD and Yvonne Dolan, MA, for being exemplars of compassion and skill as they articulate the theory/practice of resolving childhood sexual abuse. A special thanks for the time they both took to review early drafts of the manuscript. I would like to thank Eileen Schick for her impressive organizational skills, efficiency in typing and retyping, and for sharing in the excitement of this undertaking. Much appreciation to Patrick Morrissette, PhD, for his editorial assistance and comments. A special thanks to my respected friend and colleague, Allen Vander Well, PhD, who inspires integrity, joy, curiosity, and compassion in learning and in living.

Finally, I would like to thank the Canadian University and College Counselling Association (CUCCA) for granting me the Professional Development Award (1994) and for their financial contribution for this important undertaking.

Introduction

It takes two to speak truth—one to speak and another to hear.

Henry David Thoreau

Until recently, we as a society have hidden from the reality of childhood sexual abuse. The societal secret is now being revealed. As the shroud of denial is lifted, individuals are more likely to be in search of solutions to the consequences of sexual abuse that have significantly affected them. The existing literature and the experiences of clients/counselors emphasize the potential impact of abuse on cognitive, emotional, social, intellectual, mental, and spiritual spheres of life.

Group therapy can serve as an important adjunct to individual therapy by providing an interactive context for healing work to take place. Due to individual differences, however, each situation must be carefully considered to determine the suitability of group work at a given point in the individual's life. In the safety of the group setting, participants have opportunities to experience connection, validation, commonality, encouragement, and new learning as they reenter the larger, healing community. The healing work enables the individual to view the past as the bearer of important learning and as a potential resource for the present. Furthermore, the future can be embraced because of the possibilities for continued growth, hope, and desired ways of being.

Living Through the Legacy

CHILDHOOD SEXUAL ABUSE:
A WORKING DEFINITION

The term sexual abuse refers to "any form of coerced sexual interaction between an individual and a person in a position of power over that individual" (Dolan, 1991, p. 1). More specifically, Bagley and Ramsay (1986) define sexual abuse as "involving either someone at least three years older or someone of any age using direct force or threat to effect at least a manual assault on the child's genital area" (p. 36), up to the age of sixteen. Implicit in these definitions is the inability of a child to give informed consent to sexual involvement due to the authority of the adult, the child's dependent and less powerful status, and the age difference between them (Courtois, 1988). The child is involved in sexual activity for the gratification of the adult's needs.

Sexually abusive behaviors range from exhibitionism to intercourse. Sgroi, Blick, and Porter (1982) note that the range typically involves a progression through the following behaviors:

(1) nudity; (2) disrobing; (3) genital exposure; (4) observation of the child; (5) kissing; (6) fondling; (7) masturbation; (8) fellatio; (9) cunnilingus; (10) finger (digital) penetration of the anus or rectal opening; (11) penile penetration of the anus or rectal opening; (12) finger (digital) penetration of the vagina; (13) penile penetration of the vagina; and (14) intercourse.

THE IMPACT OF CHILDHOOD SEXUAL ABUSE

For individuals who experienced the victimization and trauma of sexual abuse, the search for solutions is often a very challenging and demanding journey. Despite the difficulties, healing is possible. People can and do heal (Dolan, 1991).

Recent researchers point to a number of psychosocial problems that are more common among adults who were sexually abused as children than among those without such childhood experiences. The researchers and clinicians have highlighted the following:

- Post-traumatic stress symptomatology—flashbacks, intrusive memories, sleep disturbances/nightmares, poor concentration, numbing/spacing out, hypervigilance, and anxiety (Briere, 1989; Briere and Runtz, 1993; Courtois, 1988; Dolan, 1991; Herman, 1992a).
- Cognitive distortions—guilt; poor sense of self; negative perceptions of self, others, and the future; and self-blame (Briere, 1989; Jehu, 1989). Briere (1992) notes that because of the individual's difficulty in discerning "whether or not she or he can refer to, and operate from, an internal awareness of personal existence that is stable across contexts, experiences, and affects" (p. 43), the individual may experience identity confusion, feelings of personal emptiness and inability to comfort self.
- Depression—negative thoughts/beliefs, self damaging behavior, self-destructive wishes, and shame (Browne and Finkelhor, 1986; Courtois, 1988; Dolan, 1991; Finkelhor, 1987; 1990).
- Problematic issues with eating—bulimia and anorexia (Briere, 1984; Hall et al., 1989; Root and Fallon, 1988; Waller, 1992).
- Disturbed relatedness—alterations in social functioning, feelings of isolation/being different, difficulty in establishing trust in others, and issues with sexual intimacy/identity (Briere and Runtz, 1987; Courtois, 1988; Jehu, 1989; Justice and Justice, 1979; Maltz and Holman, 1987; Westurlund, 1992).
- Physical/somatic symptoms—gastrointestinal and respiratory effects, nausea, rectal discomfort, pain, muscular tension, and stress problems such as migraine headaches, substance abuse, and hyperalertness (Browne and Finkelhor, 1986; Courtois, 1988).

According to Browne and Finkelhor (1986), the psychological impact of childhood sexual abuse and its behavioral manifestations in adulthood are linked to the pattern of "traumagenic dynamics" that is involved in childhood sexual abuse. These dynamics are organized as follows:

- Traumatic sexualization refers to the ways in which a child's sexuality is shaped in "developmentally inappropriate and interpersonally dysfunctional ways" (Browne and Finkelhor, 1988, p. 63). An example to illustrate this would be the adult who evokes sexualized responses from the child in exchange for gifts, special privileges, or rewards.
- Stigmatization refers to the perpetrator or others placing blame, a sense of being bad, or shame or guilt on the child. For example, the perpetrator may use pressure in an attempt to keep the abuse a secret.
- Betrayal by someone whom the child trusted (e.g., trusted parent or guardian who did not take protective measures after the child disclosed the abuse).
- Powerlessness that is experienced when the child's desires or attempts to stop the abuse are responded to with further threats, coercion, or manipulations by the abuser or others.

A comprehensive overview of the traumagenic dynamics in the impact of child sexual abuse, along with details of the psychological impact and behavioral manifestations, is provided by Finkelhor (1987). This framework provides a heuristic context for understanding the treatment dynamics involved with adults who have experienced childhood sexual abuse.

BETWEEN WELLNESS AND PATHOLOGY

Individual differences shape and are, in turn, shaped by the experiences of initial and long-term effects of childhood sexual abuse. The following descriptions of the resulting impact of childhood sexual abuse are not meant to be exhaustive nor do these necessarily represent the experiences of all those who have been victimized as children.

Some researchers assert that sexual abuse does not inevitably produce severe and extreme psychological problems in childhood and adulthood. Moreover, some individuals who have survived sexual abuse appear to experience less trauma than others. Some have gone beyond their victimizations and report few (if any) long-term consequences (Briere, 1989; Browne and Finkelhor, 1986).

Constable (1994), in her comprehensive review of the existing literature, notes that difficulties in psychological functioning increase when the following are involved:

- Childhood sexual abuse involving fathers/stepfathers (Finkelhor, 1979).
- Intercourse vs. fondling or noncontact abuse (Briere, 1988).
- Use of force (Finkelhor, 1979).
- Duration of abuse (Briere, 1988).
- Degree of bizarreness such as the use of sexual torture, multiple perpetrators, and satanic rituals (Briere, 1988).

Thus, it appears that the more severe the abuse, the more severe the symptomatology. Furthermore, Constable (1994) highlights the factors that have served to moderate and protect individuals against the negative effects of childhood sexual abuse. Several common factors have been identified in the lives of those who do not experience significant problems in their cognitive, sexual, or psychosocial functionings as adults. These factors include the following:

- Social support (Conte and Schuerman, 1987).
- Maternal support such as believing the child's story and taking action against the perpetrator following disclosure of sexual abuse (Everson et al., 1989).
- Resilience or positive self-concept and sensitivity to the internal states of self/others (Gilgun, 1990).
- The role of secure attachment relationships during infancy and early childhood in consolidating protective personality characteristics and in developing supportive relationships in adulthood (Luthar and Zigler, 1991).

The existing research underscores the multiplicity and heterogeneity of factors associated with the effects of childhood sexual abuse. With this picture in mind, the group counseling context needs to acknowledge the participants' realities and experiences in the most validating and self-honoring ways. The experiences of victimization and suffering must be respectfully heard. Furthermore, it is important that the group process assists the participants in accessing the strengths and resiliencies that have enabled healthy living to occur.

CHILDHOOD SEXUAL ABUSE
AND UNIVERSITY/COLLEGE WOMEN

University or college life is often experienced as a time of rapid changes and challenges. Some typical characteristics of this period include academic pursuits, competitive achievements, career life planning, the discovery/expansion of a new network (students/faculty, staff), and the exploration of relationships and intimacy. Kaplan, Gleason, and Klein (1991) state that late adolescence is a crucial period for the development of a woman's core relational self-structure. This development includes the following planes: (1) an increased potential for entering into mutually empathic relationships characterized by being able to share one's own affective states and to respond to the affect of others; (2) relational flexibility, or the capacity to permit relationships to change and evolve; (3) an ability and willingness to work through relational conflict while continuing to value the core of emotional connection; and (4) the capacity to feel more empowered as a result of one's inner sense of relational connection to others.

Childhood sexual abuse is commonly reported in college populations. Researchers have noted prevalence rates ranging from estimates approaching 16 percent (Sedney and Brooks, 1984), to lower rates of 13.4 percent for familial abuse and 10.0 percent for nonfamilial sexual abuse among women in nonclinical, college samples (Harter, Alexander, and Neimeyer, 1988). In a more recent study of 300 clients seeking help at a university counseling center, Stinson and Hendrick (1992) found that a history of childhood sexual abuse in approximately one-third of those coming to the center for personal therapy.

For women with a history of childhood sexual abuse, typical developmental issues and the built-in demands of academic life such as the capacity to learn, memorize, study, research, and concentrate can be further complicated by the consequences of the past. Difficulties with sense of self, the experience of shame, and feelings of isolation, depression, and anxiety can affect the development of women's academic, social/relational, and personal horizons (Axelroth, 1991). Given the context of academic demands, coupled with childhood sexual abuse histories, the provision of relevant individual and/or group counseling services is necessary to promote healing and academic success.

THE NATURE OF CHANGE IN THERAPY

One of the most intriguing challenges in counseling work with individuals with a history of childhood sexual abuse is to understand the process of recovery and healing. As noted, a considerable amount of knowledge has been amassed with respect to the symptoms and effects of childhood sexual abuse. This knowledge, in turn, strengthens the development of a wide range of treatment modalities. One of the existing needs at present is an examination of the recovery process from the perspective of adults who have been dealing with the effects of childhood sexual abuse.

Recent research by Constable (1994) has resulted in the development of a theoretical framework for understanding the change process. Using a qualitative method of data collection and analysis, Constable interviewed nine women and two men who had been in therapy for dealing with issues stemming from histories of childhood sexual abuse. Constable's (1994) results shed light on the ingredients of change within the counseling context. The findings have particular relevance with respect to the nature of group work for adult women with histories of sexual abuse.

A therapeutic environment that ensures a sense of safety, security, acceptance, validation, and respect can promote change. Constable (1994) summarizes the therapist attributes and behaviors that were identified in her research as being helpful in sustaining the therapeutic environment:

- The acceptance of personal experiences and accompanying feelings.
- The ability to convey understanding.
- The capacity to demonstrate care and attentiveness to the needs of the individual.
- The communication of support and encouragement.
- The affirmation of the individual's efforts to regain a sense of being in control.
- The communication of respect for the choices made by the individual.

In addition to the qualities and attributes of the therapist, Constable (1994) emphasizes the importance of the individual's experience of strengthening. This development is linked to the consolidation of internal resources; the challenge of past representations of self stemming from the context of abuse as a child; and taking risks to be connected with oneself. The strengthening of self refers to:

- The capacity to become more self-aware with respect to identifying feelings and needs.
- The cultivation of the capacity to nurture and care for self.
- The development of self-confidence and self-trust.
- The development of self-acceptance.

Although the process of recovery described by the participants in Constable's study is recursive and nonlinear, there are some similarities to existing conceptualizations. According to Herman (1992b), for example, the three stages of recovery include "safety," "remembrance and mourning," and "reconnection." Parallels can be drawn between Herman's stages and the participants' descriptions of recovery as outlined by Constable (1994) in Figure 1 and in her comments:

> The elements described as "making connection" and "building internal resources" clearly relate to the establishment of safety. "Reconnecting dissociated experience" and "understanding differently" involve the exploration and integration of memories and the resolution of dealing with the effects of being abused as a child on one's functioning in the present, learning

new skills, exploring new possibilities, and "recreating the self" in the present. (p. 227)

Figure 1 underscores the experience of recovery as being a gradual process that occurs over time. Recovery is influenced by such interacting factors as making connections (e.g., establishing a therapeutic relationship), developing internal resources, and making changes. This framework also sheds light on the vital role of group therapy in the healing process.

One of the challenges in developing a group is to incorporate creative and effective ways to attend to the identified ingredients of change. The group facilitators and participants need to find ways to sustain the components that promote recovery, healing, and hopefulness for continued change.

FIGURE 1. Elements in the Process of Recovery

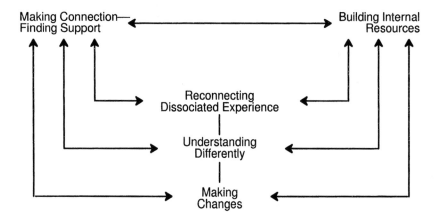

Group Work:
The Rationale and Potential Benefits

Where language and naming are power, silence is oppression,
is violence.

Adrienne Rich, 1977

Breaking silence can be a difficult and formidable process for
individuals who have experienced sexual abuse. In order to pave a
pathway for the naming of the oppression and for healing, there is a
need for a context in which these individuals can safely explore and
express both sides of their truths. There is the voice of pain, victimization, and loss, and the voice of survival, resourcefulness, and
inner wisdom.

The provision of group treatment, in conjunction with individual
therapy on a concurrent or consecutive basis, is one of the most
effective means for resolving sexual abuse (Carver et al., 1989;
Courtois, 1988; Parks and Goldberg, 1994). The group setting may
counter and alleviate some of the effects of sexual abuse. As Courtois (1988) notes, group work "allows for the breaking of the
secrecy, isolation, and stigma resulting from the abuse and fosters
exploration and resolution of the trauma and its aftermath" (p. 244).
Group therapy is potentially useful if it provides safety, understanding, and support for the individual (Courtois, 1992).

Van der Kolk (1987) highlights the strengths and weaknesses of
individual therapy, and advocates for group work when available
and appropriate. The potential role of group work in the healing
process is highlighted in the following summary:

> Most trauma victims benefit initially from individual ther-
> apy. It allows disclosure of the trauma, the safe expression of
> related feelings, and the reestablishment of a trusting relation-

11

ship with at least one other person. Patients can explore and validate perceptions and emotions and experience consistent and undivided attention from one other individual. Provided that a degree of safety can be established in the individual therapy relationship, a trauma victim can begin dealing with both the sense of shame and the vulnerability . . . Individual therapy allows for a detailed examination of a patient's mental processes and memories that cannot be replicated in a group therapy setting.

In individual therapy there is an inherent inequality: it is a relationship between a therapist, the "helper," who implicitly has answers and is not helpless, and the patient or client, who needs help and who may experience at least some passivity and possibly some sense of hopelessness. . . . Supportive individual therapy tends to reinforce dependency on the therapist and may decrease the subjective sense of mastery. (pp. 162-163)

An environment of understanding and support in a women's group can be a vital and effective resource for the beginning or continuation of the healing journey. The literature on group work is delineated for the purpose of this manual into three categories:

1. group work as a general therapeutic framework;
2. group work with women; and
3. group work with women who have experienced childhood sexual abuse.

With respect to the potential gains of group work, Brigham (1994) suggests:

1. it is a forum for expressing feelings;
2. social support, whether it is given or received, is a healing experience;
3. different opinions and conflicts can be channeled and managed in healthy ways; and
4. hope is instilled.

Writing from a relational approach to group work, Fedele and Harrington (1990) highlight the ways in which women's groups can promote mutually enhancing relational contexts. The relational approach, as developed by the clinicians/researchers at the Stone Center, Wellesley College, provides an important foundation in the development of the group sessions. Some mention is therefore warranted.

The relational model of women's psychological development includes the following:

- Women's senses of self are grounded in making and maintaining relationships with others.
- Women develop through their experiences in mutually created and mutually sustained empathic relationships.
- Empathic relationships foster a sense of energy, a capacity to act, a sense of self-worth, and a desire for further connection.
- The focus of psychological development revolves around the validation and consolidation of strengths rather than on deficits and pathology.

As noted by Fedele and Harrington (1990), women's groups can enable individuals to "work through previous relational wounds within a sustaining relational context. Both the 'there-and-then' and the 'here-and-now' relational experiences play key roles. As the woman experiences the juxtaposition of the hurtful past and the affirming present in a relational context, healing proceeds" (p. 3). Drawing from the work at the Stone Center (Jordan et al., 1991), Fedele and Harrington (1990) propose four curative factors in women's therapy groups. While these factors are not exhaustive, their importance needs to be underscored.

1. Validation as a healing factor:

   - Connections which validate, heal.
   - Both the "working through" process and the opportunity to share the pain of the past in relationship foster healing.

2. Empowerment as a healing factor:

   - Power arises out of and promotes connectedness.
   - A group context enables its members to value and encourage each others' abilities to be effective.

3. Self-empathy as a healing factor:

- Cultivates the ability to have compassion for oneself.
- The affirmation of the individual's capacity for empathy with others is highlighted along with ideas as to how these empathetic qualities (e.g., respect and compassion) could be extended to the self.

4. Mutuality as a healing factor:

- Women's groups can provide places to share and validate experiences of painful, disconnecting experiences such as abuse.
- Participants experience the consolidation of their ability to listen and act without being judgmental, to self-disclose, to allow others to have an emotional impact, to watch other members survive and forge onward, and to have courage to take responsibility for their own personal risks.

THE BENEFITS OF GROUP WORK WITH WOMEN WHO EXPERIENCED CHILDHOOD SEXUAL ABUSE

A comprehensive rationale for group treatment, entitled "Group Treatment," is by Courtois (1988). The benefits of group work, adapted by Sprei and Unger (1986), are listed as follows:

- Identification with other members and establishing a therapeutic alliance with them.
- Recognition of commonalities among members.
- Acknowledgment of the abuse and the subsequent breaking of unhealthy secrets.
- Provision of a support network and "new family."
- Exploration of emotions and beliefs.
- Provision of a safe context and catalyst for challenging beliefs and childhood messages.
- A safe place for grieving.

Other benefits are noted in the literature as well. McBride and Emerson (1989) state that group members have the opportunity to learn self-acceptance and self-assertion, to create space for trusting themselves/others, to risk in relationships, and to experience more fulfilling lives in general.

With an orientation to solutions and to the future, Gilligan and Kennedy (1989) address the common consequences of sexual abuse such as guilt, boundary difficulties, and self-abusive behaviors. It is their contention that individuals who have experienced sexual abuse tend to feel cut off from the world around them. This isolation, in turn, perpetuates a sense of "differentness" from others and a perception that something is very "wrong" with them. Such misperceptions further magnify problems, as reconnection with a larger, healing community is inhibited. Group work provides a context wherein women can break down these barriers.

The group approach taken by Gilligan and Kennedy (1989) emphasizes the following components:

- groups enable intense experiences to be explored in a larger, healing community;
- there is potential for experiences to be depathologized and normalized as individuals witness how their experiences have also been shared by others;
- groups can have a part in fostering a sense of cooperation in the change processes; and
- participants are viewed as "peer therapists" who work with each other to establish a balance between "reclaiming inner environments (e.g., the ability to feel full bodily comfort and security) and improving social skills (e.g., how to negotiate intimacy with another person." (p. 10)

The Nature of Language: Hindrance or Healing?

Lying is done with words, and also with silence.

Adrienne Rich (1979),
On Lies, Secrets, and Silence

According to Belenky et al. (1986), language serves as a necessary tool for the representation of experience; without language people remain isolated from the self. The question of whether or not one can escape from the structure imposed by language is a crucial one. According to Frank and Treichler (1989), the examination of language, itself, is a fundamental beginning point. They note that:

> Language thus no longer serves as the transparent vehicle of content or as the simple reflection of reality but itself participates in how that content and reality are framed, apprehended, expressed, and transformed. For feminists, who seek to understand the nature, scope, and mechanisms of discriminatory social practices, these issues have become pressing. . . . Anyone who explores and seeks to change women's place within texts must confront questions of women's place within both linguistic and material reality. (p. 3)

With this spirit in mind, the language used in the book for group work with women necessarily considers the use of words and speech that represent, record, and validate the lives of women. Typically, the lack of attention to language results in the marginalization of the individual. Minimal attention is given to the journey toward healthy living. In essence, a significant portion of women's lives is rendered nearly invisible due to the common discourse phenomenon in which various forms of sexual violence are represented in the public language through words created by the perpetrators of violence rather than by those who are victimized by this violence (Gannett, 1992). The importance of this phenomenon is poignantly expressed by Frank and Treichler (1989) in their comment, "[L]anguage, like other social institutions and value systems, does not serve all its speakers equally, for not all its speakers contribute equally to its formulation and maintenance" (p. 15).

From the standpoint of feminist therapy, the growing awareness and political activism in response to sexual violation includes the continuous process of speaking out, naming realities, finding voice and reclaiming space at personal and political levels (Anderson and Gold, 1994). In this light, these questions need to be asked: Who is perceived and recognized as having a voice? Who possesses the power to name the reality of women who have been sexually abused? On what basis is this reality then defined? The answers to these questions inevitably shape and are shaped by our work as counselors. By wrestling with these questions and by examining the assumptions, meanings, and implications of the language used in the counseling context, the possibilities for empowerment, understanding, and collective voices can be heightened.

FROM VICTIM TO SURVIVOR IDENTITY?

The naming of an experience such as sexual abuse has typically incorporated the language of "victim" and "survivor" (Courtois, 1988; Davis, 1990; Dolan, 1991; Gilligan and Kennedy, 1989). Such language can be viewed as advantageous as it has lifted the shroud of secrecy, silence, and isolation. There is power in naming. Moreover, the naming of experience is regarded as one of the necessary steps of the healing process. For example, as the victimization experience is identified, its impact is explored, and steps in the healing process are gradually taken. The individual acknowledges the presence of inner strength and the ability to cope. These resources may have existed well before the counseling process itself. As a result, personal and political changes can be realized.

Implicit in the use of victimization language is the existence of a perpetrator. With respect to sexual abuse, a pathological, abhorrent act is initiated by an adult perpetrator against an "innocent and uninvolved victim" (Trepper and Barrett, 1989, p. 16). While there may be little debate about the experience of victimization, more attention needs to be drawn to the underlying assumptions of this linear view and to the implications these may have for clinical intervention. There are advantages and limitations associated with the victim-perpetrator model. Although Trepper and Barrett's (1989) outline addresses father-daughter incest specifically, there is merit in recognizing some of the benefits and problems of this model:

Benefits

1. Responsibility is placed on the parents and particularly on the offending father.
2. The feelings and experiences of the children are acknowledged.
3. The father has to face the consequences of legal action.
4. Treatment frameworks that are common are used along with resources that are there in place.

Problems

1. There may be strong feelings that are experienced between family members, despite the abuse. This model does not attend to these feelings. Practitioners who subscribe to this model may directly or indirectly impose their own negative feelings about the father onto the family. The feelings of the family may not be congruent with the therapist.
2. This model is not particularly effective in accomplishing its own goals. At times, the family's wish to remain together is at odds with the counseling intervention of removing the father from the home. Being incarcerated does not automatically imply that treatment will take place for the father. If the father is not jailed, there are limits on how his absence from the home can be enforced.
3. It is also possible that in separating the father from the rest of the family, the family members can experience further disempowerment, a sense of incompetence, and inability to effect change on their own. (Trepper and Barrett, 1989 after Larson and Maddock, 1984)

One of the growing challenges is the need to reexamine the appropriateness of survivor language as it is applied to individuals who have experienced childhood sexual abuse. As a part of an identity, the survivor label views a woman's sense of self in relation to the history of sexual abuse as well as the aftereffects. Anderson and Gold (1994) note that this kind of labeling places feminists in a position of "replicating a traditional mental health paradigm" (p. 7). As feminist counselors, Anderson and Gold (1994) offer several reasons for reexamining the survivor labeling process:

1. Not all individuals have experiences that "fit" the victim/survivor framework.
2. To label someone as a "survivor" may involve the reduction of women's experiences "into categories, of attaching assumptions to the categories, and using the assumptions as primary operating principles in the therapeutic context" (p. 8).
3 The process of applying labels reduces women to a single aspect of their existence, that is, the sexual abuse.
4. The word "survivor" can be a strength as well as a limitation.

By placing primary importance on the abuse that has been suffered, a woman's identity becomes rooted in the abuse. That is, "in the process of making the abuse suffered visible, other facets of women's lives and experiences may be rendered invisible" (Anderson and Gold, 1994, p. 12).

Clearly, the language of survivorship is double-edged. On one hand, it can pave a pathway for healing through personal and professional interventions. On the other hand, the labeling process can reinforce a stigmatized and disempowered identity. This kind of generalizing can exacerbate the view that oppression is the same for all women, at all times, and in all places (Stanley and Wise, 1983).

NAMING THE GROUP: BEYOND SURVIVAL

Becoming a survivor certainly is better than being a victim, but becoming a celebrant of life seems to us to be an even better outcome. (Walters and Havens, 1993, p. 16)

That controversy and disagreement exist with respect to the use and implications of labels is sufficient reason to begin with the voices of the women themselves. The name given to the group is *Beyond Survival: Discovering Pathways to Healing*. The search for language that captures the experience of moving beyond survival is a challenging and ongoing one. Clearly though, the participants themselves have acknowledged the hopefulness and sense of empowerment that are inherent in *not* being statically labeled as survivors.

An examination of the dictionary meaning of "victim" sheds some light on this discussion. According to *Funk & Wagnalls* (1976), the word "victim" refers to "one who is killed, injured, or subjected to suffering" (p. 1493). The word "survive" means "to live or continue beyond the death of another, an event; to remain alive or in existence" (p. 1349). For some women, such definitions suggest a lack of progression and at best, a basic level of existence. This does *not* deny the experiences of victimization and survival. It is essential, however, to acknowledge the experiences of many women who no longer fall into one or both of these categories. The words "beyond survival" more accurately reflect the process of healing that continues to occur as inner strength and resourcefulness are reclaimed. In this manner, there is an explicit and implicit acknowledgement of the victimization experience as associated with temporal factors. There is little debate over the importance of creating a counseling context that promotes the open confrontation of childhood abuse and the exploration of the impact it may have on current life functioning. In the provision of therapeutic work for adults who experienced childhood sexual abuse, Trepper and Barrett (1989) caution against the tendency to focus exclusively on past abuse in their comment:

> . . . the abuse was not the only event in the adult survivor's life, and all of her existent adulthood behaviors are not a function of that abuse. Each of the client's systems must be taken into account when developing a treatment plan lest she be forced to remain in the role of the victim. (p. 243)

WHEN LANGUAGE AND EXPERIENCE RESONATE: A LOOK AT THEORETICAL FRAMEWORKS

Traumatic experiences can disrupt or shatter one's sense of self. Moving beyond survival and discovering pathways of healing are often formidable challenges. For some individuals, a victim life story can be adopted and be reinforced by interactions with others. For example, individuals may perceive themselves as having little power to make choices that influence their life situation. Over time they can maintain the internalized belief that they have little ability to experience a sense of agency in circumstances outside of the traumatic experiences (Adams-Westcott, Dafforn, and Sterne, 1993). How can new stories be created that are empowering and life-enhancing rather than disempowering and oppressing? In addition to the feminist perspective outlined, there are several theoretical models that have influenced the structure and form of this group for women. These modalities provide the foundation of the group and therefore warrant mention.

A. The Erickson Approach

(For more information, refer to "The Milton Erickson Story," presented in Session One.)

- People already have the resources necessary to live satisfying and meaningful lives.
- At some level, people know what they need to do.
- Therapy and therapeutic strategies can assist individuals in discovering motivation and accessing confidence to utilize their strengths and to pursue goals.
- Emphasis on resources.
- Respect for a multidimensional perspective working with the "whole client system" (conscious and unconscious, verbal and nonverbal, active and passive, metaphors, symbols, stories, and ceremonies) (Combs and Freedman, 1990).
- Future orientation.
- Encouragement of positive ways of being and of life-enhancing thoughts, activities and experiences, rather than using therapy to identify and cure problems.
- Focus on the wellness paradigm and the importance of directing attention to pleasure, mastery, competence, and optimism (Walters and Havens, 1993).

B. Solution-Focused Therapy

- Emphasis is on the active use of the individual's present life resources and images of future goals and possibilities.
- Individuals possess the inner resources and strengths to construct effective solutions to their issues.
- Solutions are co-created by the therapist and the client.
- Construction of solutions involve a joint process between therapist and client.
- Search for exceptions to the problem situation (de Shazer, 1988 and 1991).
- Once the facts of the victimization narrative have unfolded, this approach offers important tools for treatment.

As a prominent therapist in the treatment of sexual abuse, Yvonne Dolan draws from solution-focused therapy and the Ericksonian approach. Because this integration undergirds the group sessions, some aspects of her work warrant mention.

1. Pretreatment Changes

As defined by Dolan (1991), this refers to an "improvement in the situation for which the client is seeking therapy that occurs between scheduling the appointment and coming to the first session" (p. 30). In the prescreening interview for group members, potential participants are invited to comment on their awareness of any present or past changes that they would like to see continue.

2. The Solution-Focused Recovery Scale

As a part of the prescreening process, interested participants are asked to complete this scale and a prescreening questionnaire. Dolan (1991) has noted that this scale is particularly useful in that it provides a context of hope and begins to shift the emphasis toward healing. The healing orientation of these questions serves as a map for the identity of surviving and going beyond survival as opposed to the identity of victimization and traumatization.

3. The Miracle Question

This technique was developed by de Shazer (1988) and later modified by Dolan (1991) in her work with individuals with sexual abuse histories. There are several essential components to this technique:

    a. Imagining that a miracle has taken place and the profound effects of childhood sexual abuse are overcome
    b. Therapy is no longer necessary
    c. Envisioning a satisfying life
    d. Noticing what perceptions/behaviors would be present
    e. Inviting the individual to notice in what ways some of these healthy behaviors/perceptions may be occurring at times in daily living

4. Constructive Individual and Systemic Questions

Constructive individual questions assist the individual to identify the specifics of her own solutions and what is deemed necessary in overcoming the trauma and the negative effects it has had on daily living. For example, Dolan (1991) provides a list of helpful questions:

- What will you be doing differently when this (sexual abuse trauma) is less of a current problem in your life?
- What will you be doing differently with your time?
- What differences will the above healing changes make when they have been present in your life over extended time? (p. 37)

Constructive systemic questions are also important in that the resources of supportive family, friends, and other meaningful relationships are identified and mobilized. Examples include:

- What do you think your (significant other) would identify as the first sign that things are improving for you? What do you think this person would notice first?
- What do you think your (friends, employer, co-workers, siblings, etc.) will notice about you as the healing changes continue? (Dolan, 1991)

C. Narrative Therapy

Relative influence questioning is a therapeutic means of assisting people to separate themselves from the problem. Central to this framework is the assumption that people encounter problems when the stories of their lives, as they or others have created them, are inaccurate or inadequate representations of their lived experiences (White and Epstein, 1990). The role of narrative in therapy is to promote the process of restorying people's lives and experiences. There are two steps involved:

1. The first step involves the application of externalizing conversations. Questions that assist individuals in mapping the influences of the problems in their lives are introduced. There is an examination of how the problems influence the behavioral, social, physical, and emotional spheres of life.
2. Through a series of questions, an invitation is extended to individuals to map their own influences in the "life" of their problems. As White and Epston (1990) note:

> Ordinarily, it is very difficult for persons to locate examples of their own influence in the life of the problem . . . the identification of the influence of the problem has set the scene for the identification of the influence of persons. Persons are less transfixed by the problem and less constrained in their perception of events surrounding the problem. This facilitates the discovery of unique outcomes. (p. 45)

Reauthoring and Restorying

One means by which reauthoring and restorying can take place is through the use of landscape-of-action-questions which White (1993) defines as questions that "encourage persons to situate unique outcomes in sequences of events that unfold across time according to particular plots" (p. 40). Examples of this kind of questioning in bringing forth the recent history of a unique outcome have been highlighted further by White (1993):

- How did you prepare yourself to take this step? What preparations led up to it?
- Just prior to taking this step, did you nearly turn back? If so, how did you stop yourself from doing so? Looking back from this vantage point, what did you notice yourself doing that might have contributed to this achievement?
- Could you give me some background to this accomplishment? What were the circumstances surrounding this achievement? Did anyone else make a contribution? If so, would you describe this?
- What developments have occurred in other areas of your life that may relate to this? How do you think these developments prepared the way for you to take these steps?

Rather than use questions with the sole intention of gathering information, there is considerable merit to using questions as an intervention. As noted by Combs and Freedman (1990), questions are a potential means of generating experience and new stories. These new stories can then "change people's ideas about themselves and about what is possible for them" (p. 295). The power of questions can be exercised in the following ways:

a. To draw attention to improvement over time. (How is your present behavior different from the past?)
b. To identify exceptions to the problem description. (In what situations do you experience a sense of hopefulness with respect to your healing journey?)
c. To experience another's point of view. (What would your significant other say about this situation?)
d. To rehearse positive experiences/events in the future. (If this step is a small but significant one, what might your next step be?)

ADVERTISING AND PROMOTION OF THE GROUP

To provide the opportunity for women to learn about this particular group, several sources of advertising may be considered:

1. University/college counseling centers
2. University/college radio and tv
3. Local newspaper
4. University/college newspaper
5. University/college health services
6. Student development center
7. Medical clinics in close proximity to counseling center
8. Students' union
9. Residence/housing department
10. University/college departments (e.g., women's studies, general studies, nursing, department deans, etc.)
11. Women's Collective and Resource Center
12 Sexual Harassment Office
13. Local hospitals
14. Community agencies
15. Community information center

After completion of group sessions, local and institutional newspapers and radio/tv stations may be approached to publish a brief write-up or highlights. In the final group session, participants may be invited to take part in the above. A mutually convenient meeting time is arranged at a later date.

It is pointed out that participation is voluntary. Any decision to refrain would be fully respected. It is also emphasized that in making the decision, one needs to consider its place in the personal healing process. Participants should sign written consent forms before any further planning. Please refer to Session Thirteen.

PRESCREENING PROCESS AND QUESTIONNAIRE

The prescreening process plays a very important role in the selection of appropriate participants. The intention is that participants will benefit from the group experience. Interested individuals are invited to contact the counseling center to obtain a brochure and a questionnaire to complete before attending the pre-screening interview. A one-hour prescreening interview is scheduled upon receipt of the questionnaire.

The questionnaire covers a number of significant areas of life. Courtois (1988) provides examples of some relevant questions in

Appendix A of her book, *Healing the Incest Wound.* Although this questionnaire is designed specifically for individuals who have experienced incest, the information can be adapted for use with those who have encountered other forms of childhood sexual abuse. The completed questionnaire facilitates discussion during the prescreening interview. For example, the information contained in the questionnaire can shed light on the degree of comfort and ease experienced by the individual when discussing the abuse and its effects.

Another important tool in the prescreening process is the use of Dolan's (1993) Solution-Focused Recovery Scale for Survivors of Sexual Abuse found on pp. 52-53. This is the updated version that is to be picked up by those interested in booking a prescreening interview. Potential participants must hand in this completed scale before they attend the prescreening interview.

A copy of the completed scale is given to each group participant in Session One as reminders of their strengths and the particular aspects on their lives where change/attention is desired. This questionnaire is particularly helpful as it provides a context of hope and shifts the focus towards healing *prior* to the first session in group. With the aim of deemphasizing pathology, this scale assists the individual in identifying signs of healing and encourages the development of a personal and unique map for recovering from the effects of sexual abuse (Dolan, 1991). On a four-point scale, ranging from "not at all" to "frequently," the individual is asked to check the degree to which certain behaviors occur. Examples include the ability to think and talk about the trauma, to adapt to new situations, to take protective measures inside and outside of the house, and to choose supportive relationships. The use of solution-oriented language builds a context of hope without denying the negative effects of sexual abuse.

While other questionnaires exist, such as "Assessing the Damage" in the much popularized *The Courage to Heal Workbook* by Davis (1990, pp. 124-125), the focus is more on the negative effects/symptoms resulting from the abuse history. For example, the individual is asked on a five-point rating scale, ranging from "always" to "never," to indicate how frequently certain experiences or feelings occur. The indicators include comments such as "I want to kill myself"; "I'm scared of success"; "Sometimes, I think I'm crazy"; and "I feel dirty, like there's something wrong with me" (Davis, 1990, pp. 124-125). Some care needs to be taken in selecting the kind questionnaire that will be used.

THE PRESCREENING INTERVIEW

Facilitating a group for women with a history of childhood sexual abuse can be a difficult and emotional challenge. The prescreening interview serves a number of important purposes. It is strongly recommended that both group facilitators be present. Each potential group member is given approximately one hour to meet with the group facilitators. This time not only provides additional information for the potential participant to consider before making a commitment to the group experience, but it also enables the facilitators to get a sense of the individual's suitability for group work at that particular time.

Courtois (1988) has outlined some questions to ask during the prescreening interview. To allow time for the potential group member to prepare for the prescreening interview, it is recommended that these questions be organized into the questionnaire. Upon contacting the counseling center, the individual is invited to come in to pick up this questionnaire and bring the completed form to the prescreening interview.

Some of the suggested questions posed by Courtois (1988) include:

- What are your reasons for wanting to join this group? What do you want to get out of the group?
- Tell us about yourself, your current life—family, school, work, friends. How are things going at the present time?
- How do you think it will be for you to disclose your sexual abuse experience in a group and to hear others discuss theirs?
- Have you been in or are you currently in individual or group therapy? Tell us about that therapy—what work is/was worked on, the therapy relationship, how you feel/felt about the therapy and the relationship, etc. (p. 257)

Comprehensive overviews of the prescreening interview are provided in Courtois' (1988) chapter on group treatment, and by McEvoy (1990). It is particularly important that group facilitators have a clear sense of the kind of criteria that will be used to include or exclude potential group members *and* how the decision will be communicated to the applicant. For example, facilitators will need to assess how the criteria will address individuals diagnosed with multiple personality disorders, borderline personality disorders, having substance abuse issues (alcohol/drugs), ongoing serious personal crises, or other special needs that will affect their abilities to be committed to the group process.

Facilitators also use this time to inform the potential participant that the group program will involve thirteen sessions. Each session will be two hours in length. Any fees/costs should also be discussed and clarified at this time.

Not all individuals benefit from group work. A woman who has recently remembered or begun to talk about her abuse history may derive benefit from individual counseling as an initial step. Dealing with other members' sexual abuse histories can be an overwhelming experience for the individual who is beginning to address her own issues of abuse.

To some extent, such factors as the sexual abuse group/training experience of facilitators, degree of group commonalities, and length of group treatment may have some bearing on the optimal conditions for effective group work. The recommendation that an individual not participate in the upcoming group needs to be handled carefully. Understandably, being excluded from a group can be experienced as a rejection. It is important for facilitators to be sensitive and open to the following:

- the interested participant's potential for group work in the future; and
- the individual's need for a more appropriate resource (other than group) and to assist in the referral process, where appropriate.

Individuals who are considered appropriate for the group are contacted by phone. Each participant is asked to bring along a journal or blank notebook and pen for the duration of the group program.

GROUP SESSIONS

Session One—
The Journey: Getting Started

INTRODUCTION

Creating an atmosphere of warmth and safety is an important consideration, particularly as the group meets for the first time. It is not uncommon for the women to experience anxiety (as well as excitement) about this initial meeting. Session One is designed and structured to enable the participants to *begin* to experience a sense of safety, trust, and ease.

Preparation Before Group

- Furniture in a circle
- Atmosphere of warmth created: lighting, wall hangings, plants/flowers, tea
- Supplies
  - blackboard/chalk or flip chart
  - kleenex
  - writing paper
  - name tags/marker
  - handouts

Welcome

- Facilitators can greet the women as they enter the reception area. To ensure that the privacy of the group is protected in the waiting room area, the facilitator can also direct the women to the group room upon their arrival.
- Provide name tags (first names only).

- Formal welcome by facilitators when all are seated.
- Facilitators introduce themselves.
- Brief introduction of the group:
  - history
  - rationale
  - goals/purposes

It is helpful to highlight the complementarity of group therapy with individual counseling work. While the latter often plays a necessary and crucial part to the women's healing journeys, there are additional benefits of group involvement. Such benefits include:

1. Opportunities to continue breaking the silence in a safe and supportive context.
2. The fostering of connections with others.
3. The validation of experiences and feelings.
4. The discovery and consolidation of resources, skills, and abilities awareness *and* learning from others in the group.
5. The experience of hope, encouragement, commitment to continued healing and life affirming choices.

Structure of the Group

- Process orientation
- Psychoeducational
- Therapeutic approach
- Semistructured format

Participants have the opportunity to explore and experience possibilities for healing through several avenues:

- Group discussion
- Mini lectures
- Structured exercises
- Guided imagery/visualization
- Journal writing

Introduction of Participants

It is strongly recommended that each participant be invited to introduce herself. While it may be common to engage in a dyad exercise where the individual introduces another participant, it seems particularly relevant for each woman to begin the group with her own voice. This step accentuates one of the central group themes "from silence to voice." After stating her first-name only, each participant is asked to share her comments for the following:

- Something about herself that she would like to share with the group (e.g., field of study, career/personal interests, and background information).
- One quality about her that is reflected in her decision to join this group.
- What it is like for her to be here.

THE MILTON ERICKSON STORY

The life of prominent psychiatrist and psychotherapist, Dr. Milton Erickson, is a portrayal of the possibilities of hope and zest for life in the face of difficulties and limitations. After polio struck Erickson he experienced a close brush with death. He subsequently endured many years of dyslexia, partial paralysis, tone-deafness, and color-blindness. Though forced to use a wheelchair after the recurrence of polio later in life, he continued to pursue life with remarkable energy, interest in others, and humor.

The following is a rather delightful and fitting story related to Erickson's experience as a teenager, which the facilitator should read aloud to the group:

Keep Them on the Road and Keep Them Going

Erickson told a story about when he was growing up. Erickson had polio when he was seventeen, but before that he was a fairly active kid who lived in a farming area in Wisconsin for much of his growing up years. He told a story about how he was with friends one time a few miles away from his home. People didn't travel very far from their homes at that point and he and his friends were unfamiliar with this area. They were travelling down a country road and a horse which had obviously thrown [its] rider ran past them. Its reins were all askew and it was very skittish. He and his friends chased the horse into a farmyard, and when they got into the farmyard, they caught the horse and calmed it down. Then Erickson announced, "I'm going to take this horse back home, back to its owner." His friends said, "We don't even know whose horse this is. How're you gonna do that?" Erickson said, "That's all right." He jumped up on the horse, told the horse to giddyup and the horse went out of the farmyard and took a right turn onto the road. Erickson spurred him on down the road. As they were riding down the road, every once in a while the horse tried to go off the road and eat some weed or some hay. Erickson just steered him back on the road and spurred him on. A few miles down the road, the horse turned and went into another farmyard. The farmer heard the commotion and came out and exclaimed, "That there's my horse. How did you know how to bring my horse home? I've never met you. You didn't know that was my horse." Erickson said, "That's right, I didn't know where to bring the horse, but the horse knew the way. All I did was to keep him on the road and keep him moving."

(From *Solution-Oriented Hypnosis: An Ericksonian Approach*, by William Hudson O'Hanlon and Michael Martin. Copyright © 1992 by William Hudson O'Hanlon and Michael Martin. Reprinted by permission of W.W. Norton & Company, Inc.)

In a sense, this story captures the essence of our group to acknowledge your strengths and resourcefulness, and validate your capacity to find the path that leads you home. You know the way. We, as facilitators, are here to encourage you to continue moving.

HONORING THE GROUP

- Go over handout on group guidelines.* Check with participants to see if other guidelines need to be added.
- Missed Sessions: If participants are unable to attend a session, ask that they please notify one of the facilitators ahead of time

---

*Handouts can be found at the end of each session.

and make arrangements to pick up handouts/complete exercises before the next session.

- If a member decides not to return to the group, encourage her to attend her final session to inform the group of her decision.
- Inform participants that the group will be closed to new members after the second session.
- Explain that there will be no formal breaks scheduled during the group sessions, except during the weeks of storytelling.
- Inform them of the location of washrooms.

LARGE-GROUP EXERCISE

Ask participants what adjectives come to mind when they hear the word, "*victim*"? Brainstorm and write participants' responses on blackboard/flip chart. Some of the responses might include:

helpless	violated	loss
fear	hurt	shame
loss of control	traumatized	pain
grieving	suffering	trapped
alienation	isolation	betrayal

DISCUSSION

A common term used for individuals who have lived through past sexual abuse is "survivor." This term is undoubtedly a vital one as it acknowledges the act or state of living/continuing beyond the experience of sexual abuse. Emphasize that each participant is a survivor, and ask the question: What adjectives come to mind when you hear the word "*survivor*"?

Brainstorm and write on blackboard/flipchart. Note that responses often reflect the differences in how the term "survivor" is viewed. Some of the responses might include:

rising above adversity	making it	working through
being labeled	struggling	gaining hope
resilient	hopeful	fighter
determined	strong	existing

Group participants may comment that while it is a vital step to consider themselves "survivors," this is not sufficient in and of itself. There is an articulated need for a language/vocabulary that encapsulates the experiences of thriving well and moving beyond survival.

Read aloud to the group the following quote:

> Becoming a survivor is certainly better than being a victim, but becoming a celebrant of life seems to us to be an even better outcome. (Havens and Walters, 1993, p. 16)

WRITING EXERCISE

Invite participants to bring out their blank notebook or journal and a pen. Inform the group that journal writing is one way to capture one's inner thoughts and feelings. It can also be a way of noting the ways in which challenges or difficulties are addressed and the experiences of personal growth and contentment. Let the participants know that there will be opportunities in the group sessions for journal writing. It can also be a useful practice to journal in between sessions.

Take about *fifteen minutes* now. Instruct the group as follows: Imagine that it is the year _____ (project five years ahead), and your life reflects how you have moved beyond survival: What would you be experiencing as growth/change in your life? (Discuss in dyads, if time is available.)

EXPLORING HOPES AND CONCERNS

Work in pairs, then with large group, for responses to the following:

- What do you hope to gain in this group?
- What are some of your concerns/fears about being a part of this group?

Encourage participants to express their thoughts. Facilitators can use a blackboard or flip chart to capture ideas, and the language of the women. Acknowledge each idea and validate. Common themes can be highlighted. Note differences as well. Check if any questions, need for information, or further comments. Responses may include the following:

Hopes

- Deal with feelings of guilt
- Risk taking
- Self-acceptance
- Affirm present strengths
- Discover new, healthier ways of reacting
- Deal with control, trust, and security issues
- Assertiveness/confrontation
- Relationships—learning more about choice and discernment
- Acknowledge and follow through with creative potential (self-confidence)
- Healthy boundaries
- Share with others
- Gain support

Fears

- Not being accepted
- Not being believed
- Being misinterpreted
- Missing school/work because of triggers
- Where to go after group ends
- Reliving memories
- Having control taken away
- Facing own feelings in a group
- Facing others' feelings in a group
- Fear of change
- Feeling weak in group

- Vulnerability
- Not enough time to change in all the areas desired
- Being overwhelmed
- Losing heart as learning is gained about profound impact of sexual abuse

HEALING SYMBOLS

The use of symbols to represent experience in the therapeutic context holds potential for powerful associations and hence, continued healing. The word "symbol" refers to the "smallest units of metaphor—words, objects, mental images, and the like—in which a richness of meaning is crystallized" (Combs and Freedman, 1990, p. xiv).

Participants are asked to bring a symbol (object, short story or poem) to the next session to reintroduce themselves to the group. This symbol is to have personal significance and serve as a reminder of each participant's continued capacity to heal.

CLOSING

- Invite each participant to choose one word that describes what she is experiencing as the session closes.
- Read aloud "I See Myself," by Judith Evangeline (poem is reprinted on p. 41).
- Ask for a group participant to volunteer to bring a poem or affirmation for the next session.

Handouts

- Honoring the Group: Important Guidelines
- Empowerment: Of Life and Living

I SEE MYSELF*

I see myself
a little girl
running
smiling
wanting approval
Chasing after life
to meet it face to face
Not really afraid
But
wondering

HONORING THE GROUP:
IMPORTANT GUIDELINES

Our part as facilitators is to provide a context of safety, support, and validation of experience/emotions. It is important that healthy boundaries as well as consistency are present. Your part in this group is to attend to the steps that you consider important to your own healing work.

- Regular attendance and punctuality.
- Commitment.
- Confidentiality of information. Exceptions to confidentiality of information:
    a) if you inform us of your intention to hurt/kill yourself or another person;
    b) a child or minor, as defined by state/provincial law who is currently being abused;
    c) if you inform the court that you are receiving counseling/ therapy, the court could subpoena the therapist or our records of your involvement in the group;
    d) if you decide to take legal action or to bring charges against us.
- Allow feelings.
- Self-responsibility: respect your own style and degree of participation.
- Respectfulness of others' opinions and views.
- Listen with respect.
- Safety: physical contact (hugs, supportive gestures, etc.) ONLY IF permission is given.
- Respect privacy.
- Other guidelines:

EMPOWERMENT: OF LIFE AND LIVING

You have the resources to heal.

You have permission to tell "the secrets."

You can break the silence and have a voice.

Your experiences of the past are valid.

You can change your relationship to your memory.

You can forgive yourself.

You can protect yourself and be strong.

Your body is your body.

You have a core of wisdom within.

Your emotions can assist you.

You can reject unhealthy relationships.

You are not to blame—grownups are responsible for their behaviors.

You can experience intimacy and enjoy your sexuality.

You can respect yourself.

You can say "No."

You can honor the things you did to survive.

You can learn new ways of coping.

You can allow yourself to experience your feelings.

You can set your own pace to work on your issues.

You can be powerful and still have important needs (e.g., needs for affection, connection, and love).

You can learn to control the connection between the abuse and your present behavior/relationship patterns.

Your abuser is responsible for the violations, not you.

You can make life-affirming choices.

Your present and future belong to you.

You can enhance your sense of belonging and community.

You can go beyond survival.

You have the freedom to chart your future.

You have a future.

You can respect your capacity to change and grow.

Session Two—
A Topography for Safety and Strength

BEGINNING

- Introduce and welcome new members, if any (note that there will be no new members after this session).
- Use name tags (first names only) to encourage group connection by names.
- Encourage participants to initiate or continue individual counseling as necessary.
- Address any questions, comments, or personal reflections.
- Clarify administrative procedures.
- Announcements (e.g., upcoming events in community, or if any member is absent due to illness or other reason).
- Invite participants to bring in poetry, quotations, small portions from readings, or drawings to share at the end of selected session—ask for a volunteer for next session.

HIGHLIGHTS

The main goal of this session is to explore the participants' understandings and experiences of safety, comfort, and security. With this being only the second group session, the goal of creating safety and trust remains vital.

HEALING SYMBOLS: LARGE-GROUP EXERCISE

In this exercise, each participant reintroduces herself to the group and describes her symbol of the capacity to heal. Examples include a letter from a trusted friend, stones, jewelry, a piece of art, plants/ flowers, certain colors, a stuffed animal, photograph, poetry, books, animals (e.g., whale, eagle, or unicorn), and places in nature.

VISUALIZATION EXERCISE:
STEPS TO RELAXATION AND SAFETY

Visualization can be a powerful technique for refining one's sense of self and making important changes in life. Healing work is optimized when steps are taken to relax the body and clear the mind of distractions. Furthermore, a sense of safety and security is important to enable inner work to be accomplished. Facilitators may wish to modify these scripts to suit the group. Facilitator guides the group through the exercise. Participants are invited to comment on what they experienced.

Examples of progressive relaxation exercises are found in the following sources (for complete source information for the following, and for similar listings in subsequent sessions, refer to the bibliography):

- *Healing Voices: Feminist Approaches to Therapy with Women* (Laidlaw and Malmo, 1990: Chapter 9).
- *Self-Esteem: A Proven Program of Cognitive Techniques for Assessing, Improving, and Maintaining Your Self-Esteem* (McKay and Fanning, 1992: Chapter 11).
- *Recreating Your Self: Help for Adult Children of Dysfunctional Families* (Napier, 1990: Chapter 3).

A conceptual foundation, instructions for using trance, and scripts that employ metaphors, stories, and direct and indirect suggestions are provided in the following sources:

- *Hypnotherapy Scripts: A Neo-Ericksonian Approach to Persuasive Healing* (Havens and Walters, 1989).
- *Hypnotherapy for Health, Harmony, and Peak Performance: Expanding the Goals of Psychotherapy* (Walters and Havens, 1993).

Participants are invited to discuss their experiences with these exercises. In this visualization exercise, the facilitator selects a relaxation script to read aloud to the group. Following the reading, participants are invited to briefly comment on their experiences. What images, feelings, sound, and thoughts were noticed?

SOLUTION-FOCUSED RECOVERY SCALE
BY YVONNE DOLAN

As indicated, this scale is completed prior to the prescreening interview. For this session, participants are provided with a copy of their responses, along with the handout, An Inventory of Healing Signs. Participants are encouraged to take ten to fifteen minutes to complete this inventory. A group discussion of the participants' responses is encouraged. This enables participants to experience a sense of validation, commonality, and hopefulness with respect to the journey toward solutions and inner strength.

To assist participants in identifying the specific areas of healing or continued growth desired, the following may be listed on the blackboard/flip chart:

Areas of Healing/Growth

- Sense of self (self-esteem)
- Feelings/emotions
- Body image
- Intimacy and sexuality
- Relationships and trust
- Family of origin
- Self-care and relaxation
- Spirituality
- Other

ACCESSING SAFETY AND SECURITY: AN EXERCISE

Invite participants to bring out their journals. This is an exercise with two components: (1) individual reflection and writing (allow approximately ten minutes for writing); and (2) discussion in dyads (allow ten minutes for discussion with another group participant). Give each participant a copy of the handout, Safety and Security. Encourage writing spontaneously from the heart.

JOURNAL TIME: LETTER TO A FRIEND

Participants are asked to bring out their journals to begin a writing exercise. Allow twenty minutes for participants to complete this exercise.

> Imagine that five years have passed since the completion of this group. You receive a letter from a close friend. In this letter, she informs you that finally, after years of turmoil, confusion, and secrecy, she is ready to acknowledge the reality of her history of sexual abuse as a child. Your friendship has endured over the years. When you made your decision to disclose your abuse experiences and to discover solutions to healthy living, she provided a listening ear and a spirit of hopefulness.
>
> Your friend trusts you. She asks you to share what you discovered and learned in your healing journey. This friend seeks your wisdom, encouragement, and direction at this crucial time in her life. What would you consider valuable to share?

CLOSING

- Ask that each participant think of a strength that will remain important as she continues on with her personal work.
- Announce next week's topic on "Boundaries."

Poetry Reading by a Participant Volunteer

Invite the group participant who volunteered from the previous session to read her poem or affirmation aloud to the group. After this reading is completed, the facilitator asks for a participant who would like to bring in a short reading for the closing of the next session. Inform the group that the reading can be something that is particularly meaningful, encouraging, or helpful that they would like to share with the group.

Handouts

- Honoring Self: Characteristics of a Healthy Group
- Solution-Focused Recovery Scale for Survivors of Sexual Abuse (should be completed prior to prescreening interview)
- An Inventory of Healing Signs (to use with above)
- Safety and Security

Readings

Facilitators communicate to the group about the importance and potential helpfulness of the selected readings outside of the group context. Participants are encouraged to read these articles prior to the next session.

- *The Courage to Heal: A Guide for Women Survivors of Child Sexual Abuse* (Bass and Davis, 1988: "The Stages" of healing, p. 59; "Breaking Silence," pp. 92-101).
- Boundaries: Where You End and I Begin (Katherine, 1991: "Boundary Violations" in Chapter Seven, pp. 86-98; "Mending Wall" in Chapter Ten, pp. 120-129).

For Further Consideration: Validating Emotional Expressions

NOTE: At times, participants express interest in having access to another room close by if overwhelming emotions are experienced. Particular care needs to be taken to discuss this option collaboratively so that understanding and respect are preserved. For some, just simply being aware of the accessibility of this room creates a sense of reassurance and added security.

A common question that is asked is whether or not the group process may exacerbate personal issues. It is often helpful to invite members who have been in previous groups to share their experiences. The facilitators can underscore the fact that there are differences between group work and personal counseling. The latter often involves a more intense and in-depth focus on the issues.

One of the core themes that relates to the above is the theme of hope. Participants do wonder if and when the abuse experience can be put in its proper context in the past so that the "rest of life," hopes, and dreams become more central. The role of group is to cultivate possibilities for hopefulness and steps toward well-being.

The techniques and kind of focus in group highlight the differences in context. While consideration needs to be given to the unique place of each individual with respect to working through the sexual abuse issues and the nature/extent of present issues, it is not uncommon for emotions to be experienced differently, possibly less intensely, in group. At the same time, intense feelings are permitted, acknowledged, validated, and viewed as integral to the healing process. Moreover, participants benefit from hearing that added understanding of their experiences and validation of the accompanying emotions play a vital part in how the personal issues are encountered over time.

Facilitators and group members cannot predict or expect future behaviors of others. The individual must be given permission to find her own voice and to discover her own pathway to healing. Nevertheless, healing CAN and DOES occur in incremental ways. Knowing this will encourage each individual to take responsibility for healthy change and to experience a restoration of personal power.

HONORING SELF: CHARACTERISTICS OF A HEALTHY GROUP

- Each person can speak and really be listened to often enough to feel a sense of ownership of the group.

- Your connection to this group enables you to feel more empowered and challenged than you otherwise would.

- You look forward to meetings as times for you, rather than as an additional obligation.

- You experience honesty inside the group. For example, you can be angry or vulnerable, joyful or content.

- Being a part of this group leads you to healthy, independent actions outside of it.

- The group provides you with a sense of pride in or validation of your own identity—without putting others down for theirs.

- You feel accepted as you are.

- The group experience broadens your thoughts and feelings. It encourages you to aspire to be better than you thought you could be.

- Over time, there is a balance between what you are receiving and what you are giving to others.

- The shared experiences and desire for change promotes a bonding or connectedness with others.

Steinem, Gloria (1992). *Revolution from Within: A Book of Self-Esteem.* Toronto: Little, Brown and Company, p. 180.

SOLUTION-FOCUSED RECOVERY
SCALE FOR SURVIVORS OF SEXUAL ABUSE

Please rate each item to the degree to which it occurs:

 0 Not at all   1 Just a little   2 Occasionally   3 Frequently

A. Able to think/talk about sexual abuse.

B. Able to think/talk about things other than sexual abuse.

C. Sleeps adequately.

D. Feels part of supportive family.

E. Stands up for self (assertive).

F. Maintains physical appearance (weight, hair, nails, etc.).

G. Goes to work.

H. Satisfied with work.

I. Engages in social activities outside home.

J. Shows healthy appetite.

K. Cares for child, loved ones, pets.

L. Adapts to new situations.

M. Initiates contact with friends, loved ones.

N. Shows sense of humor.

O. Interested in future goals.

P. Pursues leisure activities, sports, hobbies.

Q. Exercises regularly.

R. Takes sensible protective measures inside and outside home.

S. Chooses supportive relationships over nonsupportive ones.

T. Able to relax without drugs or alcohol.

U. Tolerates constructive criticism well.

V. Accepts praise well.

W. Enjoys healthy sexual relationship.

X. Has long-term friendships.

Y. Satisfied with relationship with spouse or partner.

Z. Partner or spouse would say that relationship is healthy, satisfying.

Other signs of recovery (please list):

Dolan, Y. (1993). *Solution-focused recovery scale for survivors of sexual abuse.* Original in Dolan, Y. (1991). *Resolving sexual abuse: Solution-focused therapy and Ericksonian hypnosis for adult survivors.* New York: W.W. Norton. Reprinted with permission.

AN INVENTORY OF HEALING SIGNS

When I look over my responses, I feel:

I have been most strongly affect in the following area(s):

The hardest areas/statements for me to acknowledge are:

I feel the most hopeful about making changes in:

I have made significant gains in the following:

I experience the most anxiety/fear about changing:

I was surprised by:

From this inventory, I learned:

SAFETY AND SECURITY

When you hear the words "safety" and "security," what experiences in your PRESENT life do you associate with these words?

In what ways are you now able to establish ways to feel safe?

(Note that there are different ways to experience safety. Safety can mean physical safety, emotional protection, or setting psychological boundaries.)

Complete the following sentences:

In order to feel safe and secure, a young child needs. . .

The people who should be responsible for a child's sense of safety and security are (list them):

As a child, you may have experienced times of safety and security. Complete the following list:

- Places
- People
- Stories or songs
- Activities/games
- Other (e.g., certain toys, make believe, or certain times of day or year)

Session Three—Boundaries: The Lines Between Self and Others

A boundary between self and not self is the first one we draw and the last one we erase.

*Ken Wilber**

An outline is not a boundary.

Florida Scott-Maxwell

INTRODUCTION

- Check with participants to see if there are questions or comments arising from the previous session. Opportunities are given to members to address any misunderstandings, questions, fears, or concerns. This invitation provides a safe context to practice open communication skills and healthy conflict resolution.
- Invite participants to share any notable experiences of change or risks that might have been taken during the past week.
- Explain the participants that the last four sessions of group preceeding the closing session will involve a focus on Mastery Themes, and distribute the Mastery Themes handout. Invite participants to begin to think of what four topics they would like to address in these four sessions. While this might seem early, group members are given ample time to consider what themes are of importance to them as the sessions proceed. Inform the group that a collaborative decision will be made at the end of the last storytelling session, which is Session Eight.

---

*Quoted in Mason, Marilyn (1991). *Making Our Lives Our Own: A Woman's Guide to the Six Challenges of Personal Change*. San Francisco: Harper, p. 65.

RELAXATION

Guide the group through this exercise, as follows:

Allow yourself to focus inward. As you begin to take a few deep and slow breaths, you can also give yourself permission to experience a sense of calm and relaxation. Each breath you breathe in can represent the taking in of air that begins to refresh your mind, cleanse out tension, create a peaceful heart, and instill a sense of confidence with respect to your capacity and resourcefulness in this journey of healing. As you breathe outward, picture yourself breathing out, letting go of any thoughts that clutter the mind, feelings that create a sense of heaviness, and experiences that might be confusing. Allow yourself to let go of those thoughts or feelings that need letting go. Notice how your body and mind are able to experience a lightness and ease as you become more relaxed, secure in your safe place, protected in whatever ways are important for you.

GROUP DISCUSSION: WHAT IS THIS NOTION OF BOUNDARIES?

Brainstorm in large group to discuss the question, "What is your understanding of the word 'boundaries' and its relevance to you?" Responses might include the following:

- Having my own space
- Privacy
- Respect for what I want or don't want
- Protection
- Acknowledgement of my choices
- Ways to stay in control
- Ways to preserve self-respect
- Setting up appropriate lines that others cannot cross

EXERCISING BOUNDARIES:
AN EXERCISE FOR DYADS

The following is a simple exercise developed by Marjorie Rand (in press) for group work.* The purpose is to enable group participants to broaden their self-awareness and learning about their own boundaries. This exercise can be done with participants seated in chairs or in a standing position. Facilitators inform participants to be observant of the full range of their senses in this dyadic exercise.

In your dyad, place your chairs so that you are seated across from your partner. Choose who will be "A" and "B." Person "A" begins by situating your chair at a distance that defines your boundary. Take note of the distance/proximity that you need in order to establish a boundary for yourself. Draw this boundary with your hand. How close or far are you from your partner? What body position is helpful in strengthening your boundary? For example, is it helpful to maintain or avoid eye contact, stand, cross your legs, or sit at a particular angle? Notice what you feel in your body. Pay attention to your breathing as you secure your boundary. What do you experience when your partner does not have a boundary? What would you like to say to your partner as you establish your space? What reminder from your partner might strengthen your experience of a boundary? Now have your partner create a boundary and make a statement that establishes her sense of space such as, "This is the space I have created for myself. If you want to be invited in, please check with me first." Are your boundaries close, overlapping, or removed from each other?

Allow five minutes for Person "A" in the dyad to debrief her experience of setting boundaries and for Person "B" to comment on what is experienced when Person "A" establishes her space. What is it like for Person "A" when Person "B" creates her own boundary? Switch roles when the debriefing is completed. Debrief exercise in large group.

Adapted from Rand, M. (in press). Self, boundaries and containment: An integrative body psychotherapy viewpoint. In C. Caldwell (Ed.). *Getting in Touch: The Guide to New Body-Centered Therapies.* Wheaton, IL: Quest Books.

Continue the exercise through the following steps:

- Now take a few moments to become relaxed in your breathing. You may want to close your eyes or focus on something as you begin to imagine and get a picture of the kinds of boundaries that are important to you. There are different kinds of boundaries that exist. Each kind communicates a different message, depending on the context or situation and the kind of relationship that exists between the sender of the message and the receiver.
- Allow yourself to reflect on what words or images come to mind when you hear the word "boundaries." Some people, for example, experience safety and security with the picture of high and impermeable brick walls. A sense of protection and clarity may be possible despite the isolation. With whom and in what situations might you choose an image that restricts entry or access? Others value creating space for some permeability and connection with others. This desire might be reflected in a row of trees, a walkover bridge, or a low wooden fence. These examples create a sense of openness and the possibility of others being allowed in the space beyond the fence or trees. With whom and in what situations might you choose the images of permeable boundaries?
- How do you experience yourself as you look closely at your boundary from within? What is it like to be the one to establish the boundary? What message would you like others to understand about you? What changes would you like to make with your boundary, with whom, and under what circumstances? Do you need connection and support; self-protection; personal safety; solace; or renewed personal strength?
- Debrief exercise in large group.

HAVING BOUNDARIES: WHAT IS IT ALL ABOUT? (MINI-LECTURE AND DISCUSSION)

Healthy personal boundaries are necessities in daily living. Boundaries provide us with a sense of safety and a blueprint for determining our interactions with others. Moreover, they inform and remind us of who we are, our rights, and responsibilities. As

McEnvoy (1990) points out, "Boundaries tell us we are unique individuals, entitled to needs and to having those needs met. Boundaries tell us we're worthy" (p. 64).

One of the key assumptions of Integrative Body Psychotherapy is the notion of boundaries and the suggestion that boundaries create the existence of the Self and that this Self is defined as "a sense of well-being, identity and continuity" (Rand, in press). While defenses are rigid and arise from the past, healthy boundaries are flexible and focused on experiences of the present.

There are personal experiences in daily living that constitute boundary violations. Invite group participants to comment on what examples come to mind. These might include the following:

- Having someone open your personal mail
- Being touched without your consent
- Receiving unwanted phone calls repeatedly
- Having your personal journal read without your permission
- Being robbed
- Having someone "root through" your bedroom
- Having a visitor insist on extending the stay at your home
- Becoming your therapist's confidante
- Being the caretaker for your parents while you are still a child

Healthy boundaries are important in all relationships. These include parent/child, counselor/client, employer/employee, professor/student, intimate relationships, and between friends. The importance of considerations toward boundaries is discussed in Courtois (1988, pp. 266-267) and Dolan (1991, pp. 211-223).

Healthy boundaries are characterized as clear, based on choice, and flexible enough to accommodate change. These boundaries provide the means by which an individual can experience connection with others as well as a sense of separateness in relation to others. As noted by Rand (in press), healthy boundaries enable two people to be in contact. There is a sense of connection while each remains separate with thoughts and feelings that are their own. There are different kinds of boundaries—verbal, physical, social, emotional, and mental.

THEMES IN MAINTAINING BOUNDARIES

Outline the following types of themes on the blackboard/flip chart:

Rigid Boundaries

- Overcontrol
- Protection
- Care taking (putting needs of others first)
- Mistrust
- Aggressive, domineering style of relating
- Keep others at a distance
- Isolation

Diffuse Boundaries

- Unassertiveness
- Camouflaging
- "Don't notice me/I will not challenge you"
- Undercontrol
- Passivity
- Withdrawal
- Do not ask for or expect anything from anyone
- Overcompliant
- Pleasing and ingratiating

In childhood sexual abuse, there is clearly a violation of personal boundaries. Discuss the many ways in which sexual abuse violates personal boundaries. Consider such areas of life as physical, emotional, social behavioral, spiritual, and cognitive.

Incest families typically have boundaries that are characterized as either too rigid, too permeable, or a combination of both (Courtois, 1988). For example, a family that is characterized by a combination of rigid and permeable boundaries may have different rules for how each family member relates to the outside world and to each other. Moreover, rigid boundaries are evident in the isolation of the family from the community. The child is faced with restrictions in activities/contacts outside of the home. At the same time, the boundaries within the family are permeable and unclear. In this situation, a child may be expected to assume the roles of confidante, caretaker, or sexual gratifier with his/her parent. When boundaries are diffuse and unclear, difficulties with self-definition and self-regulation result (Courtois, 1988, p. 266).

Healthy interaction and communication patterns in the group and in relation to others in general involves consideration of the following:

- The development of trust
- Ways to determine others' genuineness and caring
- Ways to receive and give support so that the pattern of isolation and denied affect is broken
- Patterns of giving and receiving attention
- Discovering healthy solutions to old patterns (e.g., learning to put oneself first instead of not asking for or expecting anything from others, or putting needs of others first)

VISUALIZATION OF A PLACE OF COMFORT AND SECURITY

This visualization is based on the notion that "an experience that vividly recalls a time of comfort and well-being is likely to re-elicit the feelings of security associated with that calm pleasant state" and that "this experience can be used to develop an associational cue for comfort and security" (Dolan, 1991, p. 100). In working with individuals who have a history of sexual abuse, the associational cue can be beneficial in the following ways:

(a) provide an alternative to other less healthy or self-destructive ways of contending with the negative effects of sexual abuse;
(b) function as an ongoing resource to enable the individual to continue on with the healing steps (e.g., to help reorient from flashbacks); and
(c) assist the individual to reconnect with much-needed inner resources. (Dolan, 1991)

Steps Toward Visualization

Beginning with the basic steps of progressive relaxation as outlined earlier, guide the group through the following steps:

1. Allow your mind to guide you to an experience in which you felt relatively calm and secure, perhaps not perfectly calm but relatively so.
2. You might ask yourself, "What do I like to do when I am not thinking about serious things? What are my favorite pastimes or hobbies?" Sometimes, people like to think of a time when they were bored or in a daydream, or simply at rest.
3. Some people like to think of a place of safety and comfort, perhaps a place in nature, a healing place.
4. You may experience comfort and security in a way that is unique and special to you. You are invited to make any adjustments you wish to make so that the experience suits you exactly—a peaceful, secure calm.
5. Allow yourself to be present in this experience of comfort. Allow yourself to use each one of your senses. Notice all the details of that experience. Notice what you see . . . the objects, colors, the natural setting, etc.
6. Notice the sounds and what you hear that provides you with that sense of comfort and security . . . perhaps it might be sounds in nature such as birds; the wind; the water; welcomed words of comfort and reassurance; gentle, serene music; etc.
7. Notice the sensations or feelings that you experience as you observe and listen . . . perhaps noticing the warmth of the sun or the sand, the soothing calm of water in a quiet brook, a gentle breeze, the texture of the vegetation, or the things that connect you to this experience of calm, quiet, serenity.
8. Notice what you can smell . . . allow yourself to discover and explore the fragrances, smells, or aromas in your experience . . . perhaps it is the fragrance of blossoms and flowers, wooded pine or balsam, the ocean, whatever your experience might be.
9. Take some time to enjoy this experience with every sense that you possess. It is comforting to know that time can be taken to enjoy what is there to be enjoyed. You may also make any adjustments along the way to further enhance this experience

of comfort and security until it is just right. Is there anything you would like to add to or move out from this safe place?

10. Take time to adjust whatever is necessary to strengthen your sense of safety and protection. Notice the kind of boundary that you might create around your place of safety and comfort . . . a strong fence, brick wall, water, having protectors like guardian angels, a wise woman, guard dogs, impenetrable glass, a circle of protective light, etc.

11. Enjoy this experience one more time, this time noticing the fullness in the experience of comfort. While you are doing this, you can select a symbol that will remind you of this pleasant experience later today, tomorrow, in the future . . . a souvenir, of sorts. Give yourself time and permission to let this symbol emerge. It might be a sight, a sound, words, an image, or a sensation from your experiences of comfort and security. Notice what this symbol is and how that feels for you.

12. It's comforting to know that you can feel free to use this symbol whenever you need to reconnect to the experience of feeling relative comfort and security.

13. As you begin to reorient to the present . . . being seated in this room, hearing the sound of my voice—you can bring back with you those feelings of relaxation, restfulness, and calm. Isn't it comforting to know that you can have experiences like this in the middle of the day and enjoy this feeling as the day continues on?

14. When you are ready, you can slowly open your eyes.

Participants may be given time to write about this experience in a journal. A discussion of participants' experiences and the symbols accessed may be helpful as well.

Comments/Questions

CLOSING

Poetry Reading

Facilitator reads aloud Judith Evangeline's, "Striving for Power Song."

STRIVING FOR POWER SONG

Raven claws
pierce burning muscle
ripped, gouged heart
the soul
        left scarred.
Raven laughs
high above Earth sorrow
sways in the cool
        of cedar bough
            and mist.
Shadows
present, past.
Phantom spirits
mingle with scent of sage
            and woodsmoke.
Drum beats. . .
Time.
Still, shadows cling.

Facilitator asks for a volunteer from the group to bring a poem/ short reading to read at the closing of the next session.

Handouts and Readings

The following are to be completed by participants outside of the group session:

- Messages: Old and New.
- Mastery Themes.
- *The Courage to Heal Workbook: For Women and Men Survivors of Child Sexual Abuse* (Davis, 1990: chapter titled, "Coping: How Did I Survive?," pp. 144-163).
- *The Resilient Self: How Survivors of Troubled Families Rise Above Adversity* (Wolin and Wolin, 1993: Chapter titled, "The Challenge of the Troubled Family," pp. 3-21).

MESSAGES: OLD AND NEW

Healthy boundaries reinforce and are reinforced by healthy messages. Messages are both implicit and explicit. The following questions provide opportunities to begin exploring the sources and power of messages in your past and present.

1. What are some old messages that contributed to feelings of doubt; guilt; shame; uncertainty about self or abuse experiences; denial; or negative emotions?

2. How did the perpetrator(s) free himself or herself from the responsibility of the abuse by the kind of messages given to you about this experience?

3. What are the sources of old, negative messages?

4. What did you do with these messages (e.g., believed them at first, told someone else, kept them secret, etc.)?

5. How did these negative messages make you feel?

6. What are some old, but positive and healthy, messages?

7. What were the sources of these messages?

8. What did you do with these messages?

9. What are the messages that you hold on to now?

10. What new, healthy messages would you like to consolidate further?

MASTERY THEMES

1. Self-assertion

2. Sense of self (self-esteem)

3. Anger

4. Power

5. Relationships with men

6. Relationships with women

7. To forgive or not

8. To confront or not

9. Guilt and shame

10. Family of origin

11. Spirituality

12. Sexuality

13. Mother-daughter relationships

14. Other ideas

Session Four—
Building Strength:
Cultivating Resourcefulness

INTRODUCTION

- Address questions/comments from previous session.
- Allow time for participants to briefly share any significant events or changes experienced during the past week.

Relaxation Exercise

Take a few moments to allow yourself to become centered and focused. Remember to breathe deeply and remind yourself, perhaps through your symbol, of the important changes that have already taken place to date. Reflect on some of the details of your place of comfort and security . . . the place, colors, aromas, sounds, and the feelings of refreshment and renewal that are associated with this experience.

Debrief Exercise—Messages: Old and New

What did you experience in completing (or not completing) this exercise? What did you learn?

One of the fundamental themes in this exercise is to acknowledge the falsehoods, myths, and lies that become a part of the message to a child. Participants often experience a sense of validation and mutual understanding in hearing that other group members also experienced similar manipulations or threats as young children or teenagers.

One of the important realities is that you are now an adult woman, in possession of resources and strengths that may not have been available to you in the past. You can take steps to move on into a healthier present and future. In doing so, you may need to relinquish the responsibility for the abuse that is or was placed upon you. It is important that you distinguish the messages that are life-affirming from the messages that are life-draining. Here are a few key questions to address:

What messages did the perpetrator use to be exempt or to free himself (herself) from responsibility for the abuse? (Brainstorm in large group.)

- Promised me candies or toys.
- It's our "secret."
- Said it was done in love.
- Told me heavy drinking was the cause.
- Sex education was his "duty" as my father.
- Said all girls my age needed the experience before dating.
- I "asked for" the sexual advances.
- Tole me I never stopped him.
- Said it was a normal part of life.
- Assured me sex was a way to help me mature.

What messages did you receive that made you feel responsible for the sexual abuse?

- I was accused of making up lies.
- I was told that I was trying to get attention.
- I was asked what I did to cause the abuse to occur in the first place.
- I was taught to always believe that adults have my best interest in mind.
- I was asked why I waited so long before telling about the abuse.
- I was not supposed to show anger or hurt.
- I was taught that sex was dirty and only dirty girls have sex before marriage.
- I believed that it was important to obey an adult in order to be a good girl.
- I was asked why I didn't try harder to stop the abuse.

Debrief Exercise—Coping: How Did I Survive?

Use blackboard or flip chart.

What coping strategies apply to your past attempts to cope?

- Isolation—keeping distance from others
- Alcohol and/or drugs
- Denial (e.g., "It really wasn't that bad.")
- Fantasy—trying to imagine that I was somewhere else during the abuse or that the perpetrator was not my . . . (e.g., father, neighbor, relative, etc.)
- Involvement in abusive relationships
- Contemplating or attempting suicide
- Delinquency
- Underachiever or overachiever in school and/or work
- Problematic issues with food (e.g., bulimia or anorexia)
- Experiencing rage at everything and everyone
- Self-blame ("Somehow, I brought this on myself.")
- Mistrust of people

What strategies reflect your capacity to cope and to be resourceful?

For example, participants may identify disclosing to parent or social services, putting lock on bedroom door, journal writing, humor, counseling, seeking refuge in organized religion, engaging in sports, attending to physical care, pursuing of career, helping others who are disadvantaged, and being a nonabusive parent as healthier ways of coping.

BEYOND SURVIVING: WHAT ABOUT THRIVING?
(JOURNAL TIME)

As an adult now, what coping strategies and resources are you able to incorporate into your efforts to strengthen yourself and to continue with healthy living? Take ten minutes to note these strategies in your journal.

(Brainstorm.) In articulating your own ideas and in listening to the group members' reflections, list three areas that you would like to strengthen in your own life.

- Self-care
- Exercise
- Spirituality
- Healthy relationships
- Breaking the silence of the past
- Acknowledging and respecting steps toward change
- Allowing feelings of anger
- Learning to be assertive
- Setting firm boundaries when necessary
- Giving self permission to relax
- Spending time in nature
- Rejecting unhealthy relationships
- Not using alcohol, drugs, or sex to "numb out"
- Engaging in a therapeutic relationship
- Having own space (e.g., no longer living with or close to perpetrator)
- Cultivating creative expression (e.g., writing, drawing, sculpting, etc.)
- Taking self-defense courses
- Becoming active in antiviolence campaigns such as "Take Back the Night"
- Assisting others who have experienced abuse/trauma (e.g., volunteer at crisis center, self-help groups, etc.)

PREPARATION FOR SESSIONS FIVE THROUGH EIGHT

Some group participants may experience feelings of anxiety and uncertainty about the opportunity to tell their stories. It is important for the facilitators to provide a rationale for the next few weeks of storytelling, to clarify questions or concerns, and to provide some additional techniques to enable each individual to be strengthened.

Telling one's story in a supportive group context can provide a powerful avenue for an individual to recognize that the abuse was not her fault. Moreover, the breaking of silence and isolation is experienced in that there are witnesses to the story being told. Courtois (1988) notes that the very act of attending a group is in and of itself "a public acknowledgement of the abuse as well as an act of disclosure" (p. 246). As others tell their stories, an individual can continue to deal with personal reactions and to work out her own experience. According to Courtois (1988) the additional benefits of disclosure in group include the following:

- counter denial, minimization, and repression; and
- make it easier for the individual to discuss her experience "on the outside" with others.

Furthermore, group storytelling can allow an individual to hear another person's story with a healthy sense of distance which in turn enables the development of new healthy perspectives (Morrissey, 1982). Nevertheless, Dolan (1991) cautions facilitators not to allow storytelling to be the only focus of the group, "lest it simply reinforce the trauma rather than assisting clients in moving beyond the constrictions of the past" (p. 29). (Go over handout, Why Telling Is Transformative.)

DEALING WITH FLASHBACKS: A MINI EDUCATIONAL PRESENTATION

The importance of continuing to mobilize personal resources during the healing journey cannot be underestimated. Individuals with histories of sexual abuse often express concerns and fears that control might be unexpectedly lost—possibly during a class lecture, at work, during the group, or at home. In addition to the resources such as the visualization of a safe, healing place, healthy boundaries, a support system, and other already established means of safety, participants are encouraged to examine ways to deal with flashbacks.

Techniques of Empowerment for Flashbacks

Individuals with histories of sexual abuse commonly describe experiences of recurring nightmares, flashbacks, and intrusive memories (Briere, 1989; Courtois, 1988). Flashbacks are normal reactions to trauma. Dolan (1991) describes flashbacks as follows:

- Very vivid reexperiencing of emotions and sensations associated with the abuse AND dissociating simultaneously from the security of the present.
- Are NOT hallucinations or psychotic experiences.
- May appear to come "out of the blue" unless the experience is examined in more detail.
- May be triggered by group work, talk shows, or movies related to the theme of abuse, certain smells, sounds, sights/images, physical gestures, and any other experiences (including non-abusive ones) that evoke feelings of the abuse trauma such as fear, vulnerability, being controlled, and overpowered.
- May involve all or just some of the senses.
- Are an unconscious response to a stimulus relating directly or indirectly to the original abuse trauma.

Additionally, flashbacks vary in intensity, duration, the degree of discomfort/anxiety that results, and the extent to which daily functioning is affected or disrupted.

It is important to emphasize the ways in which a sense of control and understanding can be regained. The handout, Techniques of Empowerment for Flashbacks, represents a four-step procedure that is both practical and helpful in depotentiating the effect of flashbacks. These techniques help the individual to manage the flashbacks as they occur and to also make sense of them afterwards. Distribute and review this handout with the group.

GIVING VOICE TO A PERSONAL STORY

Distribute and review the handout, Giving Voice to a Personal Story, then invite two participants to volunteer for next week's storytelling session. Allow the volunteers to decide which of them will make the first presentation to the group.

CLOSING

- Ask each participant to name one quality or characteristic about herself that is being rebirthed or recreated.
- Poetry reading by participant.

Handouts

- Giving Voice to a Personal Story: Some Guidelines
- Techniques of Empowerment for Flashbacks: Four Steps
- Strategies for Dealing with Flashbacks
- Why Telling Is Transformative

GIVING VOICE TO A PERSONAL STORY:
SOME GUIDELINES

- Take time to reflect on what is important for the group to understand about your sexual abuse history. The avenue(s) you use to communicate to the group is flexible. For example, you may choose to write out your experience, speak from the heart, read a poem or short story that you wrote, or share your drawing(s). The important thing to keep in mind is that you give yourself permission and freedom to express your experience in the ways that best represent you.

- Be as specific as possible. There will be differences among group members with respect to how accessible detailed memories are to each individual and what is selected to share with the group. Try not to compare yourself or judge your experiences in relation to others. Your experiences are valid in and of themselves.

- Share what you are comfortable with sharing.

- Give yourself thirty minutes to tell your story and allow approximately twenty minutes for feedback from the group.

- Remember to include strengths, resources, and aspects of your healing history as well! For your personal benefit, you may consider bringing your symbols of security and safety as reminders to remain grounded in the present as you tell your story.

- If possible, bring a photograph of yourself that represents the time of the sexual abuse. Bring a recent photograph of yourself that captures a positive quality about you now. "Photographs are footprints of our minds, mirrors of our lives, reflections from our hearts," says Weiser (1993, p. 1).

- The role of the group is to provide a context of supportive listening during the storytelling and a context of supportive feedback after the storytelling.

- Giving voice to your personal story is an act of courage and inner strength. Take time to acknowledge this step with a gift to yourself (e.g., flowers, a relaxing bath, a favorite book, or an evening of listening to music).

TECHNIQUES OF EMPOWERMENT
FOR FLASHBACKS: FOUR STEPS

1. Have you felt this way in the past? What circumstances or situations did you encounter the last time you felt this way?

2. How is the present situation and your past situation similar? For example, are there particular colors, objects, sounds, locations, seasons of the year, times of day, or sensations that are in some way similar to a past experience when you felt this way? If there is one or more persons involved, how is this situation similar to the past situation?

3. How is your present situation different from the situation in the past that you are reminded about? In what ways is your sensory experience, current life context, and personal resources different from the past? In what ways is the setting different? If another person or persons are involved, what is different from the person(s) in the past situation?

4. What steps, if any, do you want to consider in order to help yourself feel better in the present? For example, a flashback may indicate that a person is once again in a situation that is in some way frightening. If this is the case, steps toward self-protection and personal security should be taken to change the current situation. On the other hand, a flashback may simply mean that a past memory has been triggered by a connection made to the past such as certain colors or odors. In such cases, messages of reassurance and comfort need to be given to the self to lessen the negative impact of past memories of trauma. (Dolan, 1991)

It is often helpful to identify practical and concrete ways to deal with the situation. Write these ideas down as resources that you can access.

STRATEGIES FOR DEALING
WITH FLASHBACKS

Maltz (1991) also emphasizes a four-step procedure as follows:

1. **STOP** what you are experiencing (if possible). For example, stop playing the music, stop the car, stop reading, etc. What is happening?

2. **CALM** yourself so that you can experience grounding and a sense of boundaries (e.g., talk to yourself, take a few deep breaths, or go to another room).

3. **AFFIRM** and reorient yourself to the present through the five senses. What do you feel, see, touch, hear, or smell in the present? (e.g., I am with my partner in my home. I am an adult, not the child that I feel like in my flashback. I can hear the reassuring words from my partner.)

4. Take **ACTION**. How do you interact or not interact with this experience (trigger) in order to feel safe? (e.g., talk to your partner, call a friend, speak with counselor, focus on being in the safety and security of the room, take time to write in a journal, or remove self from the situation such as not watching the movie on abuse.) (Maltz, 1991)

WHY TELLING IS TRANSFORMATIVE

- You become less isolated as you deal with the secrecy and shame of abuse.

- You can acknowledge the reality of the abuse.

- You create the possibility for receiving help and compassion.

- You gain awareness of your feelings.

- You can view your experience and yourself from the perspective of an understanding supporter.

- You open yourself up to healthy relationships.

- You situate yourself as a person in the present as past issues are dealt with.

- You join a community of women who possess the courage to give voice to their suffering.

- You participate in ending child sexual abuse by breaking the silence that sustains it.

- You become a model for others who have survived abuse.

- You make changes that promote inner pride and strength.

Adapted from Bass, Ellen and Davis, Laura (1988). *The Courage to Heal: A Guide for Women Survivors of Child Sexual Abuse*. New York: Harper & Row, p. 95.

Sessions Five Through Eight— Giving Voice to a Personal Story

SESSION FIVE

Introduction

- Take five to ten minutes for group members to relax and focus. A few relaxation techniques may be introduced to facilitate an atmosphere of connectedness and safety.
- The intensity of the group process and emotional content of Sessions Five through Eight potentially places demands on the facilitators. It is particularly helpful to arrange for one facilitator to attend to the process of the storyteller while the other facilitator monitors the group observations and interactions during the sessions. These roles can be switched as the second storyteller begins. This arrangement should be discussed prior to each group session.
- Co-facilitators briefly summarize the last four sessions and highlight the emphasis on

    (a) defining sexual abuse;
    (b) exploring the words "victim" and "survivor" as well as the need to find terminology that captures the steps of going beyond survival;
    (c) identifying perpetrator responsibility and the unhealthy messages around the sexual abuse that can be released as healing continues; and
    (d) mapping past and present strengths, assets, and resources

These sessions will be devoted to the importance of giving voice to each participant's experience of sexual abuse. For some, the storytelling in the group context might represent the first time that silence is being broken. Others may have had previous opportunities to tell their stories—with a parent, sibling, trusted friend, relative, another group, or with a counselor. It is important to bear in mind that the segments of storytelling may have been shared before participation in the group. Moreover, there are likely to be further opportunities for individuals to continue telling their stories long after this group has ended.

There are a few guidelines to keep in mind as the sharing begins:

- There will be a ten-minute break after the first story is completed.
- Participants are reminded to wait until the telling of the story is finished before making any comments or asking questions. The focus remains on the storyteller so that her experiences are honored and validated. In this way, the group communicates that she has been heard and believed.
- Facilitators ask that before each woman tells her story, she indicate what may be needed from the group. Examples include the request for feedback and others' perspectives to put blame and guilt in context; to have someone sit close to her; to be physically comforted; to have the group quietly acknowledge the experience of pain and sadness; or to hear the group's validation of the strengths reflected in childhood. The fostering of mutual respect, understanding, resourcefulness, and support are important considerations.
- The group is reminded that they need not take responsibility for the emotional responses experienced by group members. This not only encourages healthy boundaries but communicates the message that emotional responses are normal and valid.

The First Story

- Refer to the guidelines provided in Session Four.
- Allow thirty minutes to tell the story, followed by twenty minutes for group feedback.
- Respect the style of storytelling. For example, some participants prefer to remain more emotionally distant as the story

unfolds while others might prefer to let feelings emerge naturally.

- Facilitators can begin with comments or questions after the story is told. This step serves as a model for the group members.
- The emphasis during the feedback time is validation of experiences, feelings expressed or not expressed, strategies for coping as a child, and the strengths reflected in the efforts to pave a pathway for continued healing.
- Pass around photographs.
- As the participant completes her storytelling, she is given the opportunity to comment on her own experience and feelings of "breaking the silence" in this group.

Break for ten minutes—to create a healthy sense of space between self and others in the group before the next story is told. This break also provides some time for members to process their own emotional reactions.

The Second Story

- Follow the same outline as for the first story.
- This format is followed for each session until all the group participants have told their stories.
- Exercises or readings during these next few sessions will be minimal or focused on strength-building.
- Encourage participants to continue with their personal journals and self-care outside of the group time.

Closing

- Ask group participants to give a few words to describe their feelings at the moment.
- Facilitator asks for a volunteer to bring a poem or short reading for the closing of the next session.
- Invite two group members to volunteer to tell their stories next week. Arrange who will make the first presentation.

Relaxation

A tape of light, classical music can be played while the facilitator reads aloud the following:

> Take a few minutes to allow your mind, heart, and body to relax. You may notice that as you begin to let your muscles experience ease and comfort, your breathing becomes a little more relaxed . . . deeper . . . peaceful. That sense of calm begins to surround you, replenishing you from your head, slowly down your neck and to your shoulders and back . . . smoothing out tension in your thighs and legs. That's right, just let yourself breathe naturally, comfortably, slowly. Let the hard work of today and thoughts about later today be set aside, safely contained, secured tightly so that you can experience a time to be centered, rooted, grounded in that place of comfort, security, and solitude. Notice the colors, sights, sounds, and aromas of your place of solitude and healing. Take a few more breaths, slowly and with that natural ease. Rest assured that you can take opportunities perhaps later today, tomorrow, this week . . . to experience these feelings again. As you begin to orient yourself to this room, the sound of my voice, and the gentle music in this room, may you also bring back with you a sense of rest . . . calm . . . and lightheartedness.

Continue reading aloud, of this story:

> The story is told about a monarch who once was the proud owner of a beautiful, pure diamond. For these reasons as well as the large size of this diamond, it had no equal anywhere. Then one day, the beauty and purity of this precious stone was accidentally marred by a deep scratch. Eager to restore the diamond, the monarch sought out the most talented diamond cutters and offered a reward for restoring the stone to perfection once again. However, no one could take away the deep scratch. Later, the monarch was approached by a gifted individual who not only promised to restore the rare diamond but to also make it even more beautiful than it was originally. Moved by the clarity and assurance contained in this promise,

the monarch entrusted the precious stone to this person's care. Time passed and the promise was fulfilled. With artistic finesse, a beautiful rosebud was engraved upon the diamond and the stem was created from what was once a deep scratch.

Just as the artist transformed the scratched diamond into a rose, when life injures us, we can also craft the damage into a beautiful design. (Wolin and Wolin, 1993)

Handout

- The Life Cycle of a Peace Rose. The facilitator reads aloud the comments at the bottom of this handout. Each participant is given this handout on green and pink paper to represent the cycles of growth.

THE LIFE CYCLE OF A PEACE ROSE

1 First petals dropping	2 More petals dropping ———	3	4 ➤	5 All petals dropped
6 Petals fertilizing earth ———————	7 ➤	8 Prune plant	9 New stock grows ————	10 ➤
11 Bud developing ———————	12	13	14 ➤	15 Bud begins to open (yellow)
16 Rose slowly opening ———	17 (yellow with pink tips)	18	19	20 ➤
21 Rose slowly opening ———	22	23 (with more pink tips)	24	25 ➤
26 Rose slowly opening ——— (3 rows of petals open but center closed)	27	28 ➤	29 Bud fully open (pink center)	/////

From *Symbol, Story, and Ceremony: Using Metaphor in Individual and Family Therapy*, by Gene Combs and Jill Freedman. Copyright © 1990 by Gene Combs and Jill Freedman. Reprinted by permission of W.W. Norton & Company, Inc.

In many ways, the life cycle of a peace rose—from the petals dropping to the opening of a pink bud—symbolizes the importance of rest, nurture, and time in our own maturity and growth.

SESSIONS SIX THROUGH EIGHT

Introduction

- Discuss any comments or questions that may have emerged since the previous session.
- Announcements.

The First Story

Procedures of Session Five can be followed.

Break (ten minutes)

The Second Story

Relaxation

Use basic scripts as outlined in previous sessions.

Closing

- Invite participants to briefly comment on their experience of this session.
- Ask for two volunteers to tell their stories for next session.
- Ask participants if anyone has a poem, affirmation, or other contribution to share for the closing of the next session.
- Ask group, "What is one area of new learning for you today?"
- Poetry reading by group participant.

SESSION EIGHT: LAST SESSION OF STORYTELLING

Repeat steps outlined for storytelling.

Mastery Themes' Choices

At the end of this session, facilitators are to seek the group's collaboration and consensus on choosing the four empowering

Mastery Themes that will be addressed in the remaining weeks. Put the list of Mastery Themes on the blackboard or flip chart (from handout for Session Three). Ask if there are other suggestions to be added to this list. For groups that are longer than twelve weeks, additional themes can be addressed:

relationships	trust
intimacy	spirituality
self-care	self-esteem
dealing with anger	assertiveness
family of origin	parenting
the perpetrator(s)	appreciating the body
forgiving self/others	guilt and shame
mother/daughter	father/daughter

Healing Exercise: Words from the "Older, Wiser Self"

This is an exercise for participants to complete at home in their journals. It is adapted from Dolan's (1991) idea that the individual will grow older and wiser.

> Imagine that you have grown to be a healthy, wise old woman and you are looking back on this period of your life. What do you think that this wonderful, old, wiser you would suggest to you to help you get through this current phase of your life? What would she tell you to remember? What would she suggest that would be most helpful in helping you heal from the past? What would she say to comfort you? And does she have any advice about how therapy could be most useful and helpful? (Dolan, 1991, p. 36)

Closing

- The session ends with participants commenting briefly about their experiences of the storytellings over the past few weeks and how they feel at the moment.
- Encourage completion of the Healing Exercise for next session.
- Poetry/short reading by volunteer.

Readings

- *The Courage to Heal* (Bass and Davis, 1988: "Anger: The Backbone of Healing," pp. 122-132).
- *The Resilient Self: How Survivors of Troubled Families Rise Above Adversity* (Wolin and Wolin, 1993: "To Name the Damage Is to Conquer It," pp. 22-48).

Session Nine—
Anger and Power:
Allies in the Making

INTRODUCTION

- Address any questions or comments from last session.
- It is not uncommon for participants to wonder about continuing to work on issues specifically related to the events of the sexual abuse history. For some, the hearing of others' stories and the telling of their own may bring other reflections and feelings to the surface. Facilitators might suggest that further work can be pursued within the context of individual counseling.
- Invite participants to briefly highlight one positive experience of the past week.

DEBRIEF EXERCISE:
WORDS FROM THE "OLDER, WISER" SELF

Do this exercise in two small groups.

- What are your experiences in reflecting on and completing this exercise?
- From the perspective of your "older, wiser" self, what is important to remember? What is new learning for you?

In large group, facilitators can ask for responses to the above questions and highlight these on the blackboard/flip chart.

READ ALOUD

Lines from a poem by a woman incest survivor (Minns, 1982):

"It is not the experience of today that drives us mad, it is remorse or bitterness for something which happened yesterday and the dread of what tomorrow will bring." (p. 23)

"We must stop the killing with ourselves, with new voices, we must say what we see.

We are the women reclaiming ourselves, healing and binding and protecting ourselves.
. . . We are the women reclaiming the children we used to be and we will never be shamed again." (pp. 28-29)

ANGER AND POWER

Introduce these topics in large group:

- How do you define anger? How do you define power?
- Ask group to make distinctions between **anger** and **rage**.
- Brainstorm. Use blackboard/flip chart to record responses.
- Rage is extreme and unfocused anger—and is often unproductive.
- Anger and power are often viewed as negative, undesirable, and unwanted emotions especially for women. The reality is that anger and power are generally experienced in some way. Another reality is the existence of myths and unrealistic expectations that perpetuate self-criticism and negative self-judgment.
- Ask group for words associated with the experience of power.

Possible definitions of power include:

- Control
- Confidence
- Unmovable
- Physical strength
- Emotional strength

Collins Dictionary (1986) definition of power is:

- Ability to do something;
- A specific ability, capacity, or faculty;
- A position of control, dominion, or authority;
- A privilege or liberty

SOME COMPONENTS OF ANGER

Anger is experienced when we perceive an external event (such as an object or person) as threatening. Anger results from the frustration of unmet expectations.

Anger, on a physiological level, involves bodily changes. Muscle tightness and an increase in blood pressure are some signs.

The following exercise is an inventory of sorts to enable a closer examination of these two qualities. Instruct participants to complete the questions as quickly as possible.

- Distribute the handout, Anger and Power: Taking Inventory. Allow ten minutes to complete responses.
- Go around the group; have participants read their responses without discussing.
- Next, guide the group through the following exercise:

Anger as an Ally

Write about a time in your life when you experienced anger as a healthy resource. What was the situation? With whom, if anyone? What was happening? How did you deal with the anger? (Allow five minutes to write.)

Write about a time in your life when you experienced anger in an unhealthy way. Describe the situation. With whom, if anyone? What was happening? How did you deal with the anger? (Allow five minutes to write.)

Power as an Ally

Write about a time in your life when you experienced yourself as being angry and powerful.

Write about a time in your life when you experienced anger and powerlessness.

What was different about the two experiences?

Anger and Power: Healthy Allies

Brainstorm ideas for expressing anger or being powerful in constructive and healthy ways. What are some examples of unhealthy and destructive use of anger and power?

THE FIVE FREEDOMS

According to the world-renowned family therapist and author, Virginia Satir, individuals need to feel powerful because it ensures the need to survive. In this way, power embodies a directed energy to either be constructive or destructive. People are choice makers, thus, responsible power is a choice (Satir, 1976). Satir advocates that the strongest position of personal power is linked to five freedoms. These are highlighted in the handout, The Five Freedoms. Distribute handout and read aloud to group.

THE VERDICT: HEALING EXERCISE

Distribute handout, The Verdict: Relinquishing Self-Blame, Restoring Dignity, for participants to complete at home. In introducing this exercise, care is taken by the facilitators to explore the appropriateness of the courtroom scenario. The experience (perhaps even of actual sexual abuse cases) of courtrooms, judges, and lawyers needs processing to ensure the value of this exercise for the individual. The facilitator also asserts to the group members that this exercise is designed to empower the participant and enable her to reclaim ownership of the present and the future. The courtroom scene, despite its cold legal connotations, has been offered as a means by which the participant can be involved most directly in achieving justice. The intention of the exercise is NOT to simply exact personal vengeance or retribution but to invite each participant to examine the ways in which the past is considered in how to live well and in healthy ways in the present or future. Participants can choose to complete this exercise on their own, with a trusted friend, or in personal therapy, prior to debriefing it in the next session.

CLOSING

- Organize a phone list of group participants. Often during the storytelling or shortly thereafter, participants experience a greater degree of closeness and connectedness. A phone list can be made and circulated for those who wish to contact each other outside of group time. The phone list is optional. Each member's decision is respected.
- Go around the group and ask each person to identify one quality about herself that reflects her capacity to assert a healthy sense of power.

Readings and Handouts

- *Making Contact.* Satir, 1976: "The Five Freedoms."
- Anger and Power: Taking Inventory.
- The Verdict: Relinquishing Self-Blame, Restoring Dignity.
- *The Dance of Anger: A Woman's Guide to Changing the Patterns of Intimate Relationships.* Lerner, 1985: "Tasks For the Daring and Courageous."
- *Women's Growth in Connection: Writings from the Stone Center.* Jordan, Kaplan, Miller, Stiver, and Surrey (Eds.), 1991: "Women and Power."

THE FIVE FREEDOMS

1. The freedom to see and hear what is here instead of what should be, was, or will be.

2. The freedom to say what one feels and thinks, instead of what one should.

3. The freedom to feel what one feels, instead of what one ought.

4. The freedom to ask for what one wants, instead of always waiting for permission.

5. The freedom to take risks in one's own behalf, instead of choosing to be only "secure" and not rocking the boat.

Satir, Virginia (1976). *Making Contact*. Berkeley, CA: Celestial Arts, p. 11.

ANGER AND POWER:
TAKING INVENTORY

Complete the following sentences with the first word(s) that come to mind.

1. To be an angry woman means

2. An angry man is

3. I feel powerful when

4. When I am angry I

5. A child that is angry is

6. A powerful woman can

7. For me to experience anger is

8. When I am angry with myself I

9. My mother's anger was/is

10. My father's anger was/is

11. When I lose power I

12. A recent experience of my own power was

13. A child's power is

14. I can reject someone when

15. When I am powerful I

16. I value the experience of power with

17. Sometimes it is easier to be angry when

18. I am most comfortable with my power when

THE VERDICT: RELINQUISHING
SELF-BLAME, RESTORING DIGNITY

You are the judge presiding over the trial of a young girl/teenager and you represent the highest court of law. This young girl happens to be the YOU of years ago. The individual(s) charged has been tried. After deliberation, weighing of evidence, including yours as first and foremost, the verdict of guilty is about to be read. As the judge, you possess the power to ensure that justice reigns with respect to the sexual abuse history that young girl was subjected to and the child-hood innocence that was taken away. Over the many years, you have found a healthy and appropriate place for the expression of your anger. This ability, in turn, has given you a sense of empowerment, inner strength, and a sense of personal conviction about the impor-tance of justice for this girl's life so that she can experience freedom from the past and live in life-affirming ways. Clearly, childhood sexual abuse is unacceptable. As from the beginning, the young girl is NOT GUILTY. From your place of safety, courage, and power, how would you address the following:

A. Who is guilty? Name or identify, if possible.

B. What is the sentence, if any, for the unacceptable acts committed against the young girl?

C. What are your feelings around sentencing? Are there some mixed emotions such as sadness, love, compassion, anger, or despair? In your opinion, what are other alternatives to sentencing?

D. In some situations, such as the context of counseling, it may be possible for the individual to receive a genuine apology from the individual who abused the child (Trepper, 1986). Typically, a considerable amount of careful planning and consideration is put forth into making this a milestone for new beginnings. If you had the opportunity to receive an honest apology from the individ-ual(s) involved in the abuse, what would be said? What would your response to this apology be?

E. As the judge, you have the privilege of delivering the final words to the young girl AND to the guilty individual(s). What would you say to each?

Session Ten—
Consolidating a Sense of Self

INTRODUCTION

- Brief relaxation exercises.
- Invite participants to spend a few minutes commenting on any notable steps or new learning that have taken place since the previous session.
- Address any questions or concerns.

DEBRIEF EXERCISE:
THE VERDICT—RELINQUISHING SELF-BLAME, RESTORING DIGNITY

- Invite general comments on the experience of completing this writing exercise.
- In large group, participants are given the opportunity to share and discuss the following:

1. The sentence.
2. The judge's words to the young girl.
3. The judge's words to the perpetrator(s).
4. The offender's apology.

MINI-LECTURE:
A SENSE OF SELF— WHAT DOES IT MEAN?

The commitment to the journey of wholeness, in general, and healing from the effects of sexual abuse, specifically, is powerfully revolutionizing. Hyde (1987) notes that in the context of safety and respect, the individual is encouraged in the following ways:

> . . . to experience the power of naming; to learn a language with which she can give voice to the full range of her life experiences, not only give voice to the secret of the abuse, but also to the full range of her potential as a woman. (p. 6)

Moreover, the cultural milieu places considerable value on independence, self-reliance, and competence. The standards of society (external authority) include myths and messages that perpetuate an inaccurate and distorted notion of what it means to have experienced sexual abuse AND what it means to be a woman. In previous group sessions, some of these myths and messages have been identified and discussed.

In addressing the topic of women's ways of knowing, Belenky et al. (1986) note the following contrasts in the development of truth that is private, personal, and intuited:

- Moving from "passivity to action."
- Moving from self as "static to self as becoming."
- Moving from "silence to a protesting inner voice and infallible gut" (p. 54). When and if this adaptive move toward awareness and utilization of inner resources for knowing and valuing occurs, the benefits are life-enhancing. By becoming one's own authority and attending to the small voice of intuition, a woman is likely to encounter the repercussions in relationships, self-concept, self-esteem, morality, and behavior (Belenky et al., 1986). Self-protection, self-assertion, and self-definition are strengthened. It is important to remember that self-concept and self-esteem are learned—typically from one's primary caretakers such as family of origin. The benefits of healthy role models or important learning can be preserved while the negative and unhealthy learning can be unlearned. Growth is possible.

Brainstorm in Large Group

> What does it mean to have a healthy sense of self (self-esteem)? How do you picture life being lived out? Kinds of relationships? Activities? View of oneself? View of others?

What makes it possible to enhance our feelings about our sense of self and self-worth is the willingness to remain open to new possibilities and to risk to discover what there is to learn and to gain. The five freedoms, as outlined in Session Nine, represent a start. According to Satir (1976) there are different parts of life that connect as a whole. A change in one part will inevitably affect the other parts. Draw diagram on blackboard or flip chart.

```
┌─────────────────────────────────────────────────────────┐
│                      COMMUNICATION                        │
│                                                           │
│  SELF-ESTEEM                                TAKING RISKS   │
│                                                           │
│                         RULES                             │
└─────────────────────────────────────────────────────────┘
```

A. SELF-ESTEEM

How do I feel about myself?

B. COMMUNICATION

How do I get my meaning across to others?

C. RULES

How do I treat my feelings? Do I own them, take responsibility for them? Or, do I put them on someone else?

Do I act as though I have feelings that I do not have, or as though I have feelings that I really don't have? What are my rules? How do these validate or invalidate self and others?

D. TAKING RISKS

How do I react to being or doing something that is new and different? Who or what in my life supports me in taking healthy risks?

How can caution play a positive role? When does caution impede growth?

Exercise to Be Done in Two Groups

Allow each group to take a minute to decide which person in the group will present the list of ideas to the larger group upon completion of this exercise. Allow groups to brainstorm for ten minutes:

What Differences Would a Healthy Sense of Self Make in the Following?

self-care	personal safety	assertiveness
relationships	parenting	sexuality
body image	social	work/school

Personal Authority

Instruct each participant to write down on a piece of paper the two areas in her life in which she would like to exercise more personal authority or power in order to strengthen her sense of self.

Each participant identifies aloud what is written and then tears up the piece of paper. A basket containing a bouquet of fresh flowers (enough for each group member) is passed to the participant as she completes this step. As she puts the pieces of paper in the basket, she takes a flower for herself. This is a small but powerful symbol that represents:

- the important place of awareness and inner resources in letting go of unhealthy aspects of one's life; and
- the seeding, opening, and flourishing of new, healthy possibilities.

SOUL CARE: A BOX

In the book, *Care of the Soul,* the author, Moore (1992) comments on the notion of the soul in the following passage:

Know intuitively that soul has to do with genuineness and depth, as when we say certain music has soul or a remarkable person is soulful. When you look closely at the image of soulfulness, you see that it is tied to life in all its particulars—good food, satisfying conversation, genuine friends, and experiences that stay in the memory and touch the heart. Soul is revealed in attachment, love, and community. (p. xi)

Care of the soul is an activity of modest care that occurs continuously. The meanings are multiple and include several things: attention, devotion, adorning the body, healing, and managing (Moore, 1992).

Encourage each group participant to find a box (e.g., shoe box) and to begin collecting items that represent examples of caring for the soul: old letters; photographs; poetry; pleasant memories; music; colors; aromas; a book; symbols of encouragement, hope, or joy; and anything else that would represent and act as reminders of soul care. Encourage each participant to keep adding to this box and to give herself permission to go through this box when she needs to reflect upon the privilege and pleasure of taking care of her soul. Items can be listed in the journal as ideas-in-progress. Ask participants to bring their lists of ideas to the next session.

Handout

- Trusting Self and Others—to be completed as homework.

Readings

- *The Courage to Heal* (Bass and Davis, 1988: "The Inner Voice," pp. 287-301).
- *Care of the Soul* (Moore, 1992: "Honoring Symptoms as a Voice of the Soul," pp. 3-21).

CLOSING

- Address any comments or questions.
- Announcements.

Poetry/Reading

Read aloud the following, quoted in Steinem (1992), p. 26:

"Happiness is self-contentedness." (Aristotle, 300 B.C.)

"Oft-times nothing profits more than self-esteem, grounded on just and right well manag'd." (John Milton, 1667)

TRUSTING SELF AND OTHERS

Complete the following sentences:

1. I trust my intuition for

2. I know

3. Trust means

4. My sense of worth in a relationship is enhanced by

5. One emotion that I trust is

6. I trust myself when

7. One benefit of listening to my inner voice is

8. One hesitation about listening to my inner voice is

9. I can trust people who

10. To become my own authority, I need

11. My sense of worth in a relationship is diminished when

12. My intuition has provided me with

Session Eleven—
Relationships and Trust:
For the Health of It

INTRODUCTION

- Review journal lists of items for attending to the soul (debrief in groups of three). In group, discuss the experience of collecting important items.
- Invite brief comments on "Trusting Self and Others" exercise. Brainstorm in large group about ideas on what constitutes a healthy relationship.

EXERCISES

Journal Time

Think about the relationships you've experienced in your life. Who is the person with whom you've had the most satisfying relationship? Allow your mind to reflect on an image of that person for awhile. Picture some of the experiences that you have had with this person. Write down some of these experiences and the qualities you value in this person.

In large group, invite each participant to comment on who this person is and identify what qualities she most values about this person.

Large Group

What characteristics do unhealthy relationships have? When is a relationship an abusive one?

MINI-LECTURE: CYCLE OF VIOLENCE

Violent or abusive behavior is often referred to as "battering." This is defined as assaultive behavior between adults in an intimate, sexual, usually cohabiting relationship. This behavior can also occur in dating relationships as well as in family contexts.

All forms of abusive behavior are essentially ways in which one human being is attempting to control or have power over another. These behaviors include, but are not limited to, the following (ask group members for additional examples of each):

    a. ISOLATION: prohibiting partner from maintaining friendships, social contacts, family ties, or other outside interests; jealousy and always wanting to be in partner's presence.
    b. PHYSICAL ABUSE: kicking, shoving, punching, slapping, being locked out of one's home, being abandoned in an unsafe place, breaking bones, murder.
    c. SEXUAL ABUSE: sex on demand; forcing sex with objects, animals, or acquaintances; demanding that partner wear more (or less) provocative clothing; insisting that partner act out pornographic fantasies; being videotaped in sexual acts against partner's wishes.
    d. INTIMIDATION: making partner accountable for every action and every minute; threats to hurt those who try to help her; threats to hurt or kill children; destroys property; threats of suicide.
    e. EMOTIONAL OR PSYCHOLOGICAL ABUSE: ongoing criticism, put-downs, mockery, sarcasm, prohibiting partner to intervene when children are being abused.
    f. ECONOMIC ABUSE: forcing partner to be accountable for every penny spent; allowing partner no money or very limited money of her own; forcing partner to hand over earnings.

Invite group comments/questions.

HEALING EXERCISE: CULTIVATING A FUTURE—
A COLLAGE (TO DO AT HOME)

According to Weiser (1993), a licensed psychologist and registered art therapist, collage is "the use of numerous images attached all together on one background so that together, they form a whole image that is itself a picture or message in addition to the visual contents of its individual component parts" (p. 29). Photographs, magazine pictures, drawings, colors, textures, prints, and shapes can all be used. In this way, collages can be free-form creations and tools of expression. Instruct participants to reflect on the following while they are creating their collages:

> Imagine in the months and years to come that healing continues to take place in your life. You become a healthy woman who is peaceful at heart and possesses inner wisdom. What are some of the signs or markers that will guide your life along this pathway? In other words, how will you know that things are better and the sexual abuse is having significantly less impact on your life?

> What will you be doing to reflect the changes?

> What will you be thinking about? What feelings would be present?

> How would the important people in your life notice the changes? How will these healthy changes manifest themselves with these people? And, in what ways will your relationships be healthy?

Facilitator informs participants to bring completed collages to the final session.

COMMUNITY RESOURCES

As the group enters the "ending" phase with one week of sessions left, it is helpful to provide a list of resources for the participants to consider as possible next steps.

- Taking a break from personal work
- Personal counseling: past and/or present themes

- Continuing education
- Women's studies program
- Volunteer opportunities
- Self-defense courses
- Self-help groups
- Other groups in college/university or community
- Interest courses
- Personal development (e.g., communication skills, assertiveness, relationship skills building, yoga, anger, self-esteem, relaxation)
- Spiritual resources
- Women's groups/organizations
- Lobbying for political change in areas such as pornography, violence, family law issues, and women's health

Readings

- "The Art of Loving." (Cohen 1991).
- "Reviewing Self-Focus: The Foundations of Intimacy." pp. 201-222; *The Dance of Intimacy: A Woman's Guide to Courageous Acts of Change in Key Relationships*, Lerner (1989).

CLOSING

- Feelings check.
- Group members often express feelings of sadness in having to say good-bye in the very near future. Concern is also expressed in terms of how responsible steps can be taken to ensure that healing continues to occur. It is important to validate and acknowledge these emotions and concerns. Allow some time for discussion of these thoughts and reflections. At this time, it may be very appropriate to discuss ways in which healing and important connections can continue after the group has ended. Ideas and resourceful learning from others' past experiences are invited to encourage a sense of egalitarianism, empowerment of each other through helpfulness, etc.

Symbols of Life: Exercise

This exercise is to be completed at home by the participants. For the next session, each individual is invited to bring in a symbol of the possibility of future healing and well-being. Facilitator notes the importance of choosing a symbol that holds personal meaning and value.

Connecting with the Future Self

Read the following with soft music in the background. Participants are encouraged to focus inward and relax, and allow themselves to remain open to new learning.

It's helpful to take a few moments, or many minutes, to reconnect with the future self. You can imagine that the future self is there with you, already nearby. Remember that to experience what it's like to *be* your future self creates a magnetic, unconscious pull that draws you toward becoming that more evolved, more mature you. It's enough to have a vague impression of the future self, or you may find that you experience this part of you vividly. The clarity of our impression will probably differ from time to time. Be sure to accept whatever you experience, realizing that each day presents a new opportunity to practice self-acceptance.

There are many ways to connect with the future self. You might imagine what it would be like to hold the hand of your future self, or to feel a supportive, reassuring hand resting on your shoulder. These are images and sensations you can draw on to increase feelings supported and reassured in any situation later in the day. It may be that, at a given time, it's more powerful for you to "see" the future self and imagine what it feels like to be that person. The important thing is to reinforce the connection with, and to rekindle your desire to become, your future self.

It's also helpful to take a moment to recall the thread that connects your heart to the heart of the future self, as well as the thread that connects you and the child within. Remember that these threads are magnetic and that one you share with the future self guides, draws you, into your optimal future. Give yourself permission to experience what that pull feels like, to imagine that you can feel yourself being drawn forward.

There are many ways to interact with your future self during this portion of your inner work, other than those mentioned above. You might want to engage in a dialogue, and ask the future self some questions. You might have a problem or a challenge that would benefit from some input. At times like these, you might allow yourself to become the future self and see the problem from the perspective of this wiser you. You can then allow the back of the mind of the future self to fill the back of your present-day mind with "memories" of how you got from where you are today to where you need to be. To do this, just give yourself a few minutes where your conscious mind just drifts or focuses on the scenery around you, as your unconscious takes in whatever the future self has to offer. Remember that the memories of the future self become the new ideas, responses, and moments of inspiration that lead you forward, today, step by step.

Also, remember to say to the future self, "I want to be you," "I am becoming you," or "I am you." You can discover other phrases that suit your experience at any given time, things to say that reaffirm your desire to become your future self.*

---

*Source: *Recreating Your Self: Help for Adult Children of Dysfunctional Families,* by Nancy J. Napier. Copyright © 1990 by Nancy J. Napier. Reprinted by permission of W.W. Norton & Company, Inc.

Session Twelve—
Honoring the Quest for Spirituality

INTRODUCTION

This session encourages participants to examine the contributions of spirituality to their continued healing and overall personal development.

Invite each group participant to briefly describe her symbol of the capacity for future healing and wellbeing. The facilitator reminds the group members to keep the symbol in a visible and accessible place so that it can serve as an ongoing reminder of the importance placed on the many aspects of healthy living. The participants are asked to bring their symbols to the closing session.

Ask the group participants what words come to mind upon hearing the word, "spirituality"? Brainstorm on blackboard/flip chart. Examples may include:

joy	faith	integrity
connectedness	beauty	belief in supreme being
wholeness	living fully	valuing life
discovering	community	inner peace
life meaning	security	God

MARKERS OF SPIRITUALITY

Journal Exercise

A. Spirituality can be an important part of one's personal journey or family story. Briefly highlight aspects of your spirituality with respect to the following time frames, as appropriate:

- childhood (infant - 12)
- teen years (13 - 19)
- young adulthood (20 - 39)

- middle adulthood (40 - 59)
- later adulthood (60+)

Include significant people, experiences, messages/beliefs, values you were exposed to, and any other important influences.

B. How was your spirituality impacted by the experience of sexual abuse?

- I regarded God as my new feather who would help me.
- I struggled to believe in God and His power to rescue me from the abuse.
- I began to pray more.
- I feared that God did not exist at all and if He did, He was not a caring, powerful God who could/would help me.
- I explored a number of religions in search of inner peace.
- I felt the protective presence of angels around me.
- I lost faith in God, my parents, everything. It was a very frightening and lonely time in my life.

Engage in large group discussion after personal journal time.

TAKING INVENTORY

Ask participants to consider the following:

- What spiritual beliefs from childhood need reexamining at this point in your life?
- What beliefs are ones that are consistent with a child's way of having faith which may be outgrown or not applicable as you move through adulthood?

THE PURPLE STONE EXERCISE

The color purple is often associated with royalty, dignity, healing, renewal, and rebirth. A basket of purple stones is passed around. Each participant is invited to take a stone.

Ask participants to take a few minutes to reflect on an aspect of their lives that negatively influences their spirituality, and to name/

identify what or who they would like to let go of or say good-bye to. Examples may include:

- I would like to let go of the hatred I have had toward myself for not doing more to stop the abuse.
- I would like to say good-bye to the paralyzing sadness of not having a chance to be a child in the true sense.
- I want to say good-bye to overworking and taking everything too seriously in my counseling work.
- I need to say good-bye to the hatred toward my father that festers within me.
- I want to let go of the eternal wish that my abuser would apologize. I have kept on hoping throughout the years and he or she is no longer alive to fulfill this wish of mine.

Next, take a few minutes for participants to consider what or who they would like to welcome into their lives to encourage healing and rebirth. Examples:

- I want to welcome times of laughter and relaxation.
- I would like the freedom to explore my faith in God once again.
- I would like to renew my hope in the future.
- I want to take more risks with my partner.
- I welcome the chance to redefine my spirituality. I can no longer have the faith of a child so I'll need a lot of time to sort things out.

MAKING ROOM FOR SPIRITUALITY

Break into two groups for this exercise. Have one person record ideas. Then engage in large group discussion.

The spiritual journey is different for each person. The purpose of exploring this topic is to enable you to clarify what is important in your life. If you were to project your life five years into the future, what spiritual resources do you hope to have cultivated in your life? What would your spiritual self be experiencing? In what practical, concrete ways might that be evident to you or others?

CLOSING

Participants are reminded to bring their symbols of continued healing and completed collages to the closing session.

Each participant is encouraged to briefly describe how she is feeling as the group prepares for the closing session. Time is given for the feelings of group members to be discussed, validated, and normalized.

Poetry Reading

ABSOLUTION*

Bless me Father,
for I have sinned
Bless me Father,
for I have sinned
Bless me
for I have
For I have sinned
sinned. . . . me
father sinned
Bless me Father
Bless me!

---

*Copyright © by Judith Evangeline. No part of this poem may be reproduced without the permission of the author.

Session Thirteen—
Celebration of Life: Cultivating
a Future and Closing Ritual

INTRODUCTION

For this final session, an atmosphere of warmth and celebration is created with herbal tea, fruit, and muffins.

Facilitators acknowledge and normalize the range of feelings and emotions that participants may experience as the group draws to completion.

DEBRIEF EXERCISE:
A COLLAGE OF CULTIVATING THE FUTURE

Facilitator briefly introduces the centrality and universality of rituals in life. While the kinds of rituals vary across cultures, their importance lies in the connection and community that can emerge from these practices. Though normally associated with cultural and spiritual practices, rituals also emerge and are acknowledged in everyday life in order to celebrate important events such as graduation, marriage, birth, festive celebrations, coming of age, and birthdays.

To begin the ritual of closure for the group, the facilitators invite each participant to bring forth the collage that she has created as discussed in a previous session. Facilitators distribute masking tape to secure collages on the walls. Each participant is then invited to display her collage and discuss its important aspects.

ACKNOWLEDGMENT OF EACH OTHER

This is an exercise that involves the participant writing down a few reflections about the qualities and strengths of each participant/

facilitator that have been valued or appreciated over the duration of the group sessions. Facilitators hand out enough index cards to be used by each group member and facilitator. For example, if there are eight group members and two facilitators, each person would receive nine index cards. Approximately fifteen to twenty minutes can be given to complete this exercise. The index cards are exchanged. Each participant is invited to take a few minutes to quietly read the written comments that have been received from the group.

Evaluation/Feedback

Distribute the evaluation handout to each participant and allow ten minutes for completion, followed by discussion of comments or highlights from group members.

Break (ten minutes)

Planning for Follow Up

- Group discussion to explore mutually agreed on date for follow-up meeting. This meeting is scheduled four to six weeks after the last session. The theme of discussion is left open-ended, unless otherwise indicated. Often group members are eager to provide an update on continued or new changes. The follow-up meeting also affords an opportunity for the group to discuss issues and concerns and to learn new strategies for further growth.
- Individuals are encouraged to continue with individual counseling to address important themes in more depth as the need arises. The option for individuals to contact the facilitators for a personal appointment is also discussed. This is particularly useful for those who want to "check in" with issues that do not require indepth counseling.
- Facilitators may discuss the opportunity for group members to share their personal experiences of being in the group with the campus or community newspaper. A consent form is handed out to those who express interest in sharing their experiences with media contacts. This form is signed and returned to the

facilitators after the arrangements are made for the interviews, and the participant is provided with the details of the media source(s) and any specific information related to the interview itself. Emphasis is placed on:

- the preservation of anonymity with respect to the information shared; and
- the importance of each participant determining for herself if this step is in the interest of healing at that particular point in time.

CLOSURE

Symbols of Life

Each participant is invited to identify again the symbol of future healing she has brought with her today. Facilitators can note the fact that as the healing continues, other relevant symbols are likely to appear as "gifts" of healthy living. As the group draws to a close, there are "gifts of symbols" that the facilitators can give to each participant. The following represent symbols which emerged as themes during the group sessions. It is particularly important that the selected symbols have relevance and meaning for the group. As Combs and Freedman (1990) note, a symbol in the form of words, objects, mental images, and the like, enables the richness of meaning to be crystallized and powerful associations to be set off.

Facilitators bring small gift bags and tissue paper so the symbols can be taken home safely by the participants. Facilitators can take turns in presenting the symbols.

- A white stone, to represent a child's innocence, purity, and strength.
- Pine, to symbolize the importance of friendship with self and with others. The pine needles represent the importance of utilizing natural and intuitive wisdom for self-protection. For example, it is sometimes necessary to reject and set limits on unhealthy relationships in order to preserve dignity and self-respect.

- A red rose, as a reminder of the story of the monarch's scratched diamond and the possibilities (the rosebud) that can be carved out of life's imperfections; or, as a symbol to represent love of one's body, mind, and spirit.
- A glass marble, to transport the mind back to times of play and laughter as children. May it be a reminder to have time to play and to take breaks from the personal work and the tasks of healing.
- Flower seeds in a packet, to symbolize the unfolding of springtime. Like the promises of growth, rebirth, and blossoming ahead, hope is eternal.

Transformation: A Visualization Script*

Once upon a time, deep in a quiet, dark forest, stood a tree. And on one of its uppermost branches there hung a curious object. It resembled a little brown silken pouch, and it hung on the underside of a high branch deep in the quiet, dark forest. The little silk pouch hung there through a long, long winter. Inside the pouch slept a quiet creature . . . sleeping, sleeping a quiet, deep sleep, its little body curled up, motionless. But all through the cold winter, warm inside its silken pouch, the little body kept growing . . . so slowly you couldn't be sure, but growing it was. As it grew bigger and bigger, the silken pouch fit more and more snugly, and held the little creature more tightly, but still the little body kept growing and growing until one spring day, it had grown so big that the silken pouch gently began to tear. As it tore, a larger and larger opening appeared in its side, until one day the pouch opened from one end to the other. The little creature stirred and felt its new space. Then cautiously, trembling in all its fragile body, it pushed its head outside the pouch. It couldn't see very much because the forest was still quite dark and its eyes were still only partly open. It could hear murmurings, and it could see soft, vague shapes; it could smell a wonderful and tantalizing

---

*From *Stories for the Third Ear* by Lee Wallas. Copyright © 1985 by Lee Wallas. Reprinted by permission of W.W. Norton & Company, Inc.

fragrance. And so, trembling, it dared to emerge yet farther and farther from within its soft, silken prison. And when at last it crept free of the pouch, it stood on shaky legs, all wet and skinny and very, very unsure of itself.

In the sky, over the trees in the forest, the sun shone brightly and the golden light filtered down through the leaves in a patchwork of shapes and patterns. There just ahead, with ever strengthening eyesight, it saw a bright shape on the bough and, lured by the shining, beautiful color, the little creature cautiously crept forward inch by inch, stopping at every small step to look about fearfully. And at last, entirely free of the little brown pouch, it moved right into the golden shape. There it felt the warmth, the warmth of the color, almost heard the vibrating sound of the golden color, and the fragrance it smelled was also golden. As the warmth spread over its body, it felt energy tingling and beginning to surge. Steadily it began to feel its strength and it stood up ever straighter, lifting its head. Then it discovered wondrous long feelers at the top of its head that could sense all around it the new world of the forest. Its heart began to swell with a feeling, and a sense almost like love, almost like power, almost like strength, almost like joy.

And as it grew warmer and warmer in the golden shape that surrounded it, it began to unfold from its body a wonderful, wonderful pair of translucent wings that kept spreading wider and wider. And on the wings there emerged a fantastic pattern of glorious color and shape and design, and the little creature trembled as it allowed its wings to flutter gently in the sunlight. As they dried, they became every more powerful until at last the little creature began rhythmically as in a dance, it began rhythmically raising and lowering its two beautiful wings. Ever more quickly, ever more powerfully, the marvelous wings beat the air until, with a surging leap into space, the little creature soared upwards higher and higher until it was flying, gliding, dipping, held up by the air, propelled forward by the strength of its wings, sailing in a graceful dance high above the forest . . . free, beautiful, and winging its own way into the welcoming world.

Handouts

- Evaluation/Feedback
- Consent Form (for media interviews)

EVALUATION/FEEDBACK

1. In general, what have been the benefits for you in being in this group?

2. What did you value the most?

3. Should the group be made longer?

4. What new ideas or topics would you like to suggest?

5. Any recommendations for change with respect to future groups?

6. Would you recommend this group to others?

THANK YOU FOR YOUR COMMENTS

CONSENT FORM

I, _____, AGREE TO BEING A PARTICIPANT IN THIS INTERVIEW TO DISCUSS MY EXPERIENCE AS A MEMBER OF THE GROUP, *BEYOND SURVIVAL: DISCOVERING PATHWAYS TO HEALING.* I UNDERSTAND THAT MY PARTICIPATION IN THIS INTERVIEW IS COMPLETELY VOLUNTARY AND THAT I MAY WITHDRAW AT ANY POINT DURING IT.

SIGNATURE _____

DATE _____

Self-Care and the Therapist:
Creating a Context for Renewal

INTRODUCTION

Psychotherapy is an expression of self-renewal. When practiced ethically and competently, both therapists and participants can benefit from this experience. Therapists can rekindle passion for personal growth, exercise creativity, renew hope, and experience insights in the art of counseling.

The definition of therapist self-care encapsulates spiritual, mental, emotional, and physical well-being (Faunce, 1990). The therapist who pursues self-care will find it possible to gain fresh perspectives, a greater sense of energy, and a spirit of connectedness with oneself, the wider community, and the universe. Moreover, therapist self-care from a holistic, preventative approach expands the opportunities for the client's growth and healthy patterns of living.

The healing power of group psychotherapy is also intricately linked to the dynamic web of human relationships. The relationships among group participants and between participants and therapists play an important role in fostering a healthy sense of well-being. Furthermore, relationships are woven into the fabric of one's personal and professional life. There are life roles and identities that extend beyond that of the client-therapist relationship. One of the most important tasks of the therapist is to cultivate a healthy sense of self amidst the myriad of responsibilities of working with individuals with past sexual abuse histories.

With the exception of the Feminist Therapy Code of Ethics (Porter, 1995), no other ethical code addresses the need to include self-care issues as an ethical imperative. Porter (1995) asserts that this inclusion is ". . . based upon a common assumption about therapy that therapist well-being is positively related to the client's therapeutic outcome" (Porter, 1995, p. 248). As indicated in the literature, ". . . doing trauma therapy can affect therapists negatively and that its effects are different from those related to doing general psychotherapy" (Pearlman and Mac Ian, 1995, p. 559). Given this reality, the ethical imperative of therapist self-care is a compelling invitation for therapists to engage responsibly and adequately in their work with clients.

This chapter highlights some of the vital aspects of therapist self-care. A discussion of the reactions and experiences of therapists to sexual abuse work is outlined. Emphasis is placed on the person-of-the-therapist, as the multidimensional components of a healthy sense of personal and professional self are explored.

SIGNS AND WONDERINGS: THE NEED FOR RENEWAL

Sexual abuse work is challenging work. Our minds, bodies, and spirits remind us of this reality time and time again. We often walk alongside our clients as they encounter the sadness, pain, regret, loss, and anger of working through their abuse. In so doing, we share these emotions at some level. As new theories and therapeutic approaches are advanced, different client and therapist responses are possible. This development, in turn, informs therapists of the need to remain abreast with the nature and extent to which they are affected by sexual abuse work. Being able to engage in self-observation and to expand self-knowledge are essential components of the therapeutic relationship. Clinical work guides and is guided by the therapist's capacity to remain attuned to self-examination and self-care. According to Porter (1995), therapist self-care is associated with three main functions. First, it protects the client by decreasing the risks associated with ethical violations, particularly ones involving power and boundary issues. Second, it enhances therapy with the client by promoting and modeling growth and well-being. Third, it protects the therapist from work-related hazards such as burnout, and from therapeutic errors by clarifying the balance that must be negotiated between the therapist caring for self and caring for others.

COUNTERTRANSFERENCE:
THE MESSENGER OF SELF-CARE

The term *countertransference* is used extensively in the sexual abuse literature (e.g., Courtois, 1988; Dolan; 1991; Pearlman and Saakvitne, 1995; Friedrich, 1990). In more simple terms, it refers to the therapist's reaction to a client which is influenced by who the therapist is and what the therapist brings to the therapy process (Friedrich, 1990). Countertransference reactions may be evoked by an event in therapy or in the therapist's life (Abney, Yang, and Paulson, 1992). A comprehensive and detailed review of counter-transference is provided by Pearlman and Saakvitne (1995), who assert that countertransference is a part of all psychotherapy and constitutes a part of each therapeutic relationship. Furthermore, countertransfer-ence contributes in several ways to the therapeutic process. According to Pearlman and Saakvitne (1995), the potential benefits of counter-transference experiences include: (1) the provision of information for therapists to inform and direct their therapeutic interventions; (2) the provision of critical diagnostic clues about the client's psychological presentation and specifically about the use of dissociation, and (3) the development of the therapist's base of self-knowledge, self-observa-tion, and empathy for the vulnerability of the client.

The therapist's responsibility is to recognize and identify personal issues that may limit effective counseling practice. Furthermore, the therapist needs to ensure that therapy remains focused on the cli-ent's needs and well-being rather than on the management of the therapist's personal issues. The therapist's inability to maintain a level of self-care may contribute to boundary violations, inappropri-ate emotional involvement, isolation, poor judgment, and power abuses (Porter, 1995).

Literature pertaining to the reactions of therapists to sexual abuse work has burgeoned over the past decade. There is recognition that a form of post-traumatic stress or a sense of secondary victimization can be experienced by the therapist (Abney, Yang, and Paulson, 1992; Dolan, 1991; Schauben and Frazier, 1995; Steele, 1991). Courtois (1988) refers to this as *contact victimization* while Fol-lette, Polusny, and Milbeck (1994) identify it as *secondary trauma-tization*.

While the actual naming of the countertransference reflects differences, the therapist's reactions include:

1. The desire to deny or remove oneself from the situation due to shame, pity, rage, dread, repugnance, horror, or being aroused or attracted to the client by his/her disclosure. There may be a sense of incompetence in not possessing the magical answers, a loss of faith, or privileged voyeurism (Courtois, 1988). A therapist may experience frustration or resentment toward a client's growing dependency, fear of becoming unhelpful, and despair over relapses and lack of progress (Goulding and Schwartz, 1995).

2. The reactivation of the therapist's feelings or relational paradigms from the past—including abuse, family-of-origin issues, and significant relationships—may be reflected in overinvestment or underinvestment in the client's therapy work (Dolan, 1991). In one example, a therapist with a sexual abuse history did not have the opportunity to face the abuser as this individual was no longer living. In supervision, the therapist noted the connection between her deep sense of *forced emotional closure* and the focus she imposed on the client to confront her own abuser while the opportunity existed. The therapist also acknowledged mixed feelings of relief and envy as she reflected upon the possibility of the client confronting her own abuser in the future.

3. The therapist's concerns in working in a group context with individuals who have sexual abuse histories include rescue fantasies; rage toward the offenders; overprotectiveness; feelings of blame toward the group member(s); frustration over the challenging, long work involved in therapy; fear of betrayal; and fear of group failure (Ganzarain and Buchele, 1986). As a result, the therapist may experience internal pressure to ensure that the clients receive optimal help during therapy. In reality, the healing process is not necessarily time-limited and may continue long after therapy is terminated. New relationships, continued learning, life experiences, and healthy changes/choices are some factors that assist individuals to place the past in its proper historical context.

4. The grief process and the specific experiences of denial, anger, sadness, and acceptance/resolution are normal responses of clinicians who hear accounts of child victimization, betrayal, and loss.

Integral to the mourning process, these emotions are natural responses that reflect a heightened capacity to work sensitively and compassionately with others (Boniello, 1990).

5. Several categories of countertransference responses are highlighted by Pearlman and Saakvitne (1995). First, there is a countertransference response to the taboo against child sexual abuse and to the eradication of the parental images as held personally and culturally. Disgust, outrage, horror, survivor guilt, and avoidance may be experienced. A second response is parental countertransference. This refers to the desire to protect the client from reexperiencing parental inadequacies, to reparent, or rescue the client in a fantasy-driven manner. A third response is the denial or inability to hear descriptions of the abuse. Denial on the therapist's part can perpetuate secrecy, dissociation, and the displacement of rage.

Therapist sexual countertransference is also likely to hinder treatment. This fourth response includes a voyeuristic countertransference whereby some aspects of the client's abuse history evoke the therapist's curiosity, arousal, or excitement as well as concomitant feelings of shame and guilt. Voyeuristic countertransference includes preoccupation with eliciting the client's description of the details of the sexual abuse experience during an initial interview. The diagnosis of multiple personality disorder for a traumatized individual may evoke powerful feelings of incompetence or anxiety, intellectual/ academic curiosity, and textbook-driven clinical impressions about the client.

Given the myriad of potential therapist responses, therapist self-care is a challenge facing professionals who work in the area of sexual abuse. The aforementioned responses provide valuable information regarding personal or professional aspects of the therapist's functioning, the client, and the therapeutic relationship. In fact, countertransference can be a resource and solution to a problem, and it can also be an important channel for insight, direction, and change (Saakvitne, 1995).

LIVING FROM THE WELL: A PARABLE

Once upon a time in a faraway land, there lived an old woman. Her secluded stone cottage in the forest was enclosed by thick towering branches of century-old trees whose shadows seemed to brush against the fuchsia-orange sky at dusk. Surrounded by tall ferns, sunflowers, morning glories, snapdragons, and daisies, the house resembled a fortress. Situated in the middle of the garden was a well of amethyst stones. A magnetic glow emanated from the well as the sun's rays refracted from these precious stones.

The woman had inherited this magical well many years earlier. To ensure its timeless existence, her benefactor instructed her to hand out the gemstones wisely and cautiously, as they would benefit the recipients. The amethyst given as a gift would serve as a symbol of hope, optimism, and courage.

News of the magical well spread across the countryside, and people from far and near journeyed to receive the woman's blessing and a precious amethyst stone to overcome a host of worries and concerns. Amethysts were drawn from the well to protect crops from hailstones, promote lovely dreams and visions, quicken intelligence, protect soldiers in battle, enhance shrewdness in business ventures, and control bad thoughts.

Crowds entered the woman's garden gates daily in search of answers and in anticipation of solutions. Some slept by the magical well throughout the night, waiting for the woman to reappear at daybreak; others returned weekly to secure more gemstones. Deeply touched by the people's reliance on her treasures, the woman came to believe that only her well of amethysts was truly magical.

As the years passed, the woman began to worry as the stones at the bottom of the well became fewer. Visitors in need began to see lines of worry crease her forehead. She lost some of her vibrancy and her step lacked the bounce of days gone by. One evening she noticed that there was only one stone left in her well. Acknowledging that her well was now depleted, she stayed in her house for weeks, not bearing to face visitors.

One sunny morning, a young woman briskly and confidently made her way through the garden to the front door of the old woman's house. Years ago, when in great need, she had received an amethyst from the older woman. Now she was startled by the dilapidated fence, the weedcovered cobbled path, and sunburnt flowers. When she knocked on the cottage door, she was surprised to see the once cheerful woman who answered looking weary and frightened.

"My dear friend, I have no more amethysts to give," the old woman mumbled in a weak voice, anticipating a request for help. The young woman replied, "Do not worry. I am not here to ask for anything; I am here to tell you I've found my own magical well of amethysts, and from it I have brought one for you. Please take it as my gift to you."

The old woman received her visitor, served a cup of tea, and listened intently to her story. She took the stone given to her and hid it in her most secret place. That evening, long after her visitor had left and no one was in sight, the old woman felt compelled to leave her house and slowly make her way back to her own well. She looked inside and admired the faint glimmer of the last remaining rock. As she drew it up toward the top she was struck by its royal purple color. Turning it over, she saw her named carved in gold! She ran back to her house with the stone clasped close to her heart, and placed it in the secret place beside the other stone. A spirit of thanksgiving and gratefulness appeared as she looked over the amethyst stones. As the harvest moon cast a warm glow over the evening sky, a new song of joy emerged from the old woman's heart.

Early the next morning, the old woman was awakened by the bright sun shining through her window, and the sound of voices calling her name. Going out and greeting her visitors, she tried to explain that her well was empty. "Come and see, the well is dry," she said, all the while thinking of the two lovely rocks safely hidden in her most secret place. "Look and see," she said, lifting the cover off the well. The visitors gathered around and suddenly began to laugh and cheer. Startled, the old woman looked in her well and saw it filled to the top with amethyst.

VIEW FROM THE THERAPIST'S CHAIR

Therapist self-care is inextricably linked to personal conceptualizations of the therapeutic process. It is helpful to examine the theoretical approaches and assumptions about change and healthy living that shape our work with sexual abuse victims. What do we consider to be the ingredients for recovery from sexual abuse? What perceptions do each of us hold about our part and the client's role in the therapeutic process? Who else plays a critical part in the client's life? How much time do we spend promoting the clients' utilization of their own resources both within and outside of the therapeutic context? In what ways do we draw distinctions between functional and dysfunctional dependency within the therapeutic relationship? Do we celebrate with clients who encounter the unexpected joys and miracles along the way, or do we respond with uncertainty and skepticism?

Therapists, at times, base their clinical work on preconceived notions. In doing so, this work is regarded as necessarily long-term with a focus on symptom alleviation, memory work, and crisis management. There may be a working assumption that clients will continue to endure the negative ramifications of their traumas until therapy is completed, if ever. Furthermore, it might be assumed that the effects of trauma have penetrated every sector of their lives. This may or may not be the case, and care needs to be taken to address the areas of life that have been least affected with the passage of time.

A closer examination of the therapist's role in the process of client socialization is critical to ethical practice. In other words, how do we responsibly guide clients as the therapeutic relationship begins and continues? Do we assume that we know significantly more about a healthy lifestyle than the client? What client image is created? What image of the therapist is created for the client? What are the possibilities and limitations of therapy?

Johnson (1995) provides an excellent description of a pattern of ineffective treatment of individuals with a sex abuse history:

> The therapist typically perceives quite correctly that the patient's defenses serve to avoid remembering and working through a traumatic event or series of events. The therapist assures the patient that she will be well once the trauma is uncovered. The patient valiantly tries to remember the trauma and in fact does recover painful and frightening memories. As that happens, the patient begins to experience dramatic worsening of symptoms, often including self-injury and a variety of panic symptoms. The patient is fearful and reaches out to the therapist, who tries to be available . . . There follows a long period of intensive therapy, again marked by uncovering of more trauma, more exacerbation of symptoms, and increasing intensity of treatment. . . . This type of pattern following the valiant and sincere efforts of the therapist leads to a general pessimism. (pp. 157-158)

This vignette illustrates the potential for a co-created downward spiral for both the client and therapist. What can be drawn from this description is the importance of recognizing the powerful choices available to therapists. As clients seek guidance, a growing trust in the therapeutic process is developed over time. One of the natural consequences is that clients behave and respond according to the therapist's formulations of them (Johnson, 1995). If the premise is held by the therapist that the client is resourceful and possesses strength to move beyond the trauma history, then the course of therapy is fundamentally different than if the client is viewed as weak and incompetent. In this sense, therapist self-care determines and is determined by how the client is viewed and responded to in the therapy context. For example, a therapist who combines a problem focus with an expert role can become overinvolved in treatment, can underestimate the client's capacity for change, and is likely to experience burnout.

As I reflect upon my counseling experiences, I am reminded of the need to remain flexible in the impressions and conclusions that are drawn about clients. At times, clients bring their issues/concerns only to the therapy context. Therapy is perceived as a time for problems to be addressed. In the more restrictive view of therapy, the client and/or the therapist is focused on the problems, worries, misfortunes, or inadequacies that have accumulated since the last therapy session. The therapy session becomes associated with the aspects of life that are problematic and the negative feelings that pertain to these experiences. In fact, therapy may also become the only time that these issues are directly addressed. The depth of the issues are known only by the therapist and the client. The nature of the relationship may in turn reinforce the sense of growing responsibility (and accompanying exhaustion) that the therapist experiences with the client. One possible response to therapy from the client's point of view is that life goes on outside of therapy. Energy is expended in maintaining a job, school demands, extracurricular activities, and relationships. For the unassuming therapist, the danger lies in viewing the client largely within a problem-oriented framework obtained in the therapeutic context. It should not come as a surprise to the therapist when the client is generally sad, vulnerable, or frustrated in the therapy room, and energetic, competent, and pleasant in contexts outside of therapy.

A second potential pitfall of this approach is the client's sense of debilitation and vulnerability that extends beyond the therapy room. Depression is reinforced, a sense of inadequacy permeates, and hopelessness is unnecessarily prolonged. Such contrasts compel the therapist to encourage a more balanced and accurate view by accessing the capabilities and competencies of the client which he or she demonstrates in daily living situations.

One of my most significant learnings about therapist self-care has its source in a client's capacity for self-care. Over a holiday season, I had been working with a client who described herself as severely depressed and suicidal. Her uncertainty about not harming herself, coupled with a minimal support network, led to our arrangement to be in touch by phone. When I contacted her home, I was surprised to learn that she was in the midst of hosting a festive party. It was evident that she was full of energy and enthusiasm. She simply stated that it would be "a real drag" to spend the holidays depressed, miserable, and isolated. Needless to say, I was very moved by her decision and her capacity to engage in self-care when I least expected it. During subsequent sessions, she acknowledged that she had experienced a sense of hope and a level of renewed energy. She also expressed confidence in that many personal struggles would be alleviated over time.

Some therapists are likely to wonder if a sudden "turn for the better" should be viewed with suspicion. With this particular mindset, the therapist may expend considerable energy in trying to reorient the client back to the identified concerns of the past, worrying about the flight into health, and anticipating a return flight into depression. Therapist self-care cannot be unaffected by the theoretical contexts and the accompanying therapist's responses to the client.

RESILIENCY: A LOOK AT THE PERSON OF THE THERAPIST

At times, out of curiosity or genuine interest, clients ask, "How are you able you keep on doing this kind of work day after day?" The common answers might be rather sanguine and polite, such as,

"Oh, I just make sure I pace myself," "The work is challenging but it is very rewarding," "The work fits with what I like to do and with who I am." These responses to the question, however, might have more to do with therapist resiliency and resourcefulness.

In general, resiliency pertains to the ability or power of springing back to an original position or form after being stretched or bent. The term also refers to the individual's capacity to deal with overwhelming adversity, to rebound from hardships, and to initiate creative survival skills. There has been a recent surge of interest in understanding resiliency in individuals who have experienced troubled and traumatic pasts (Higgins, 1994; Valentine and Feinauer, 1993; Wolin and Wolin, 1993). While this literature has relevance for therapists on a personal level, it is not specifically written to address the self-care of therapists who work with individuals who have experienced childhood sexual trauma. In other words, what enables therapists to continue doing effective, ethical work in the area of childhood sexual abuse? How are the resilient capacities constructed and sustained? In what ways do therapists attend to their own need to go *beyond survival* as helping professionals? Answers to these questions have more to do with a healthy life style than simply drawing up a list of strategies or behavioral prescriptions.

The cartography of therapist self-care contains markers of self-preservation and renewal. Self-care is often a personal journey reflecting the uniqueness of each therapist. The mosaic of markers includes a blend of the technical-concrete, philosophical-abstract, and personal-professional aspects of self-care. Embedded in this journey is challenge and mystery as the developmental nature of self-care involves the interweaving of time passages with life experience, faith in one's capacity to change, and a passion for participating in one's own growth and that of others.

CULTIVATING SPIRITUALITY

Central to self-development and self-care is the capacity to nurture one's own spirituality. The notion of spirituality has its Latin roots in *spiritus,* with its meaning linked to words such as breath, life, and alive (Merwin and Smith-Kurtz, 1988, cited in Phillips and Frederick, 1995). According to Pearlman and Saakvitne (1995), spiritual damage (e.g., difficulties in connection, meaning and hope, awareness, and the nonmaterial) result from trauma and vicarious traumatization. These authors highlight the restorative qualities of the following:

Connection

To counter the spiritual damage of vicarious traumatization, a sense of connection with something that extends beyond oneself is important. This might mean cultivating a sense of history, community, or belonging to life itself. Connection with a higher power or nature, or participation in religious activities such as prayer, meditation or yoga are examples.

Meaning and Hope

Clinical effectiveness is also influenced by the therapist's own restoration of hope, joy, and meaning in life in the face of the client's story of pain. This aspect of spiritual renewal is unique and personal. It refers to the therapist's ways of sustaining hope in the personal sphere of living. Examples include self-reflection, honoring certain guidelines for living, and engaging in activities that are more clearly unrelated to the trauma of others.

Awareness

As the therapist becomes aware of the depth of pain and suffering of those who experienced childhood sexual abuse, consideration also needs to be given to the strengths and survival skills that the client demonstrates in order to manage her life amidst abuse. Rather than focusing narrowly on victimization, the therapist can attend to the client's resiliencies or what is considered to be *learned resourcefulness*. Outside of the therapeutic context, the therapist can take measures to further renew spiritual strength. Limited exposure to childhood traumas and human suffering on TV, radio, or in newspapers can be a means of conserving emotional and psychological energy for clinical work.

Nonmaterial

Therapist renewal is connected to how joy, beauty, and love are incorporated into life. Work with sexual abuse victims, by its very nature, addresses aspects of humanity that pertain to sadness, portray ugliness, and perpetuate hate. The therapist's pursuit of activities, people, or experiences that reflect goodness and love helps to counter the deleterious effects of trauma work.

ATTENDING TO THE SOUL

Therapist self-care is not so much about eliminating countertransference responses. It is more about ongoing care or attending to what is being communicated through the body, mind, and soul. It means opening oneself to examining reactions in the therapeutic context and drawing upon what can be learned, and to see how personal and professional growth can be promoted.

Milton Erickson's notion of utilization has application for therapists in terms of attending to the soul. At the core of this concept is the belief that therapists already have all the resources they need to live satisfying and meaningful lives (Combs and Freedman, 1990). The therapeutic context serves as the ground for countertransference responses and needs to be regarded as a container of resources. It is also a tool for understanding (Pearlman and Saakvitne, 1995). In terms of therapist self-care, the emphasis is on the therapist's utilization of *symptoms* or countertransference responses.

The phrase, *honoring symptoms as a voice of the soul*, as coined by Moore (1992), has relevance regarding the concept of utilization. Moore (1992) states that the soul is not about a thing, but the relatedness, value, heart, depth, and personal substance of experiencing life and ourselves. To begin with, it is essential to *go with the symptom*. For example, a therapist who experiences sadness and helplessness after hearing stories of personal trauma in the group therapy session may be enriched by respecting the presence of these emotions. What is needed is the capacity or permission to oneself to listen and look attentively at what is being communicated through these feelings. In this particular example, the therapist identified the powerful emotions that were tied to her personal need to do something to obliterate the group members' childhood losses. Rationally and theoretically, she recognized the impossibility of meeting this need. However, on an emotional level, feelings of ineffectiveness and self-doubt were initially pervasive throughout the group sessions.

Becoming more attuned to her perception of sexually abused individuals as *always victims somehow*, weak, and incapable of overcoming adversity, the therapist began to take active steps to dispel these myths. Over time, she acknowledged that she was better able to hold a place for these emotional responses and discover therapeutic ways to access the members' sadness and helplessness, as well as their tenacity and strength in moving beyond survival. Furthermore, the therapist became more attuned to her pattern of viewing the group of women as they were in the past—young, vulnerable girls. This awareness became a source of important personal and professional growth for the therapist. The following comments capture and underscore the importance of honoring our symptoms as therapists:

> When people observe the ways in which the soul is manifesting itself, they are enriched rather than impoverished. They receive back what is theirs, the very thing they have assumed to be so horrible that it should be cut out or tossed away. When you regard the soul with an open mind, you begin to find the messages that lie within the illness, the corrections that can be found in remorse and other uncomfortable feelings, and the necessary changes requested by depression and anxiety. (Moore, 1992, p. 6)

THE PRESERVATION OF SELF

Realizing that therapists involved in childhood sexual abuse work experience varying levels of disruptions in their personal and professional lives, comes as no surprise. The challenge is to find ways of attending to oneself that are effective and personally relevant. The literature addresses a range of issues under the rubric of self-care. Included are books that address the general topic of professional burnout (Grosch and Olsen, 1994; Kottler, 1993), compassion fatigue and secondary traumatic stress disorder (Figley, 1995; Pearlman and Saakvitne, 1995), and the specific self-care concerns in sexual abuse work (Bell-Gadsby and Siegenberg, 1996; Crowder, 1995; Friedrich, 1990).

Self-care necessarily entails a holistic perspective. The following points represent some questions for consideration during the course of therapeutic work with sexually abused individuals and has relevance for therapists both within and outside of the counseling context.

MATTERS OF THE MIND, BODY, AND SOUL

Professional Knowledge and Skills

- What knowledge base equips you to work in the area of sexual abuse?
- What are the philosophical assumptions underlying your conceptualization of the impact of sexual abuse on an individual and how healing/recovery takes place?
- How much counseling experience have you had with the issue of childhood sexual abuse?
- If you were to articulate your theory of trauma and recovery, what would you consider to be important ingredients? In individual counseling? With couples? With families? In the group context? Outside of group?
- What are your sources of professional training and preparation for this work?
- In your view, what favorable conditions in the client's life might contribute to a shorter length of therapy? What conditions would you regard as warranting intensive therapy?
- What professional markers inform you that self-care needs have been attended to?

Group Practice

- What is your experience with groups for individuals who have experienced childhood sexual abuse?
- What is your role in the group?
- In what ways does the therapy group reflect your theoretical perspective(s)?
- What are the purposes of the group program?
- How compatible are you with the co-therapist? Theoretically? Where do the differences seem most apparent? Personally?
- How many sessions are involved in the group therapy program? What is the length of each session?

- How is each session planned/debriefed between co-therapists?
- In what ways are the session topics arranged to recognize the realities inherent in the negative sequelae of abuse AND individual resiliencies and victories?
- What is it about the group's content and structure that contributes to client AND counselor renewal?
- What are the delimitations of the group? In other words, what will the group NOT necessarily provide or focus upon?
- If you are working in an agency or organization, how many staff are available to facilitate a therapy group for individuals with a sexual abuse past?
- What other counseling issues does your work include? If you were to estimate a percentage breakdown of an average work week, what proportion is related to sexual abuse work, other clinical issues, other types of counseling-related work such as career or academic counseling, training, supervision, professional development, administration, or teaching?
- What are your sources of personal renewal and rest after your group session is completed?

SUPERVISION

- If you are a supervisor for therapists working in the area of childhood, what is your own model of supervision? Is there supervision of supervision available?
- Is supervision available to you to help address issues that arise in your individual counseling? Is it available for your role as a co-therapist in a group?
- In what ways is the supervisory context a place where you experience some ease in discussing countertransference responses? How often do you receive supervision?
- Are there other professionals such as a peer group who can offer consultations?
- In terms of therapist self-care, what do you hope the supervisor or consultant would encourage you to consider? What do you need from supervision?

- If you are supervising, what strategies for self-care have you implemented for your professional preservation and growth?

THE PERSONAL SELF

- According to Moore (1996), "The soul has an absolute, unforgiving need for regular excursions into enchantment" (p. *ix*). Moore likens enchantment to a spell; an aura of fantasy and emotion that can comfort the heart, add charm, and provide refreshment; and a condition that enables us to connect intimately with others.
- What places, people, activities, or things create a sense of enchantment in your daily life?
- In what ways do you experience a sense of community?
- What would you consider as significant times of pleasure, peace of mind, or serenity?
- Outside of the work context, what are your sources of joy, laughter, well-being, and rest?
- What avenues have you created to address your personal concerns and issues?
- How do you debrief from your role of therapist at the end of the day?

CULTIVATING AN ATTITUDE OF SELF-CARE

Learned Resourcefulness

"Abuse is a plague that should occasion universal sorrow. Miraculously, some of its victims do not lose their radiance" (Higgins, 1994, p. 317). What is it about the lives of these individuals with an abusive past that reflects the emergence of strengths and capacities over time? What is it that enables some individuals who have experienced devastating trauma to be resilient enough to overcome these adversities while others continue to struggle? In a recent study, resilient individuals shared the following common commitments: a tendency to protect their time for reflection, to approach potential problems proactively, and to hold on to the belief that their lives will improve if they take charge and put forth effort into the issue at hand (Higgins, 1994).

A significant proportion of therapy time is often taken up with the individual's experience of pain and victimization. Such an emphasis is a timely and necessary part of therapy. However, there needs to be time set aside to explore the particular ways in which the individual initiated steps of self-protection, mustered strength to forge ahead, took risks to alter the direction that the abuse-related events imposed upon them, or triumphed over the raging internal battles of the past. Therapists can be helped by the clients to learn more about what the healing process entails, to identify the strengths of the past and present, and to identify the strategies that will further the departure from the victimization experience. The absence of this exploration perpetuates a sense of learned helplessness in the client and pessimism in the therapist. The client may either leave therapy prematurely or remain in therapy with feelings of uncertainty and hopelessness.

At times, therapist self-care may be compromised by the misguided belief and practice of dichotomies, such as: the client is weak and the therapist is strong. It is important that clients learn more about living a healthy life, which can be facilitated by the therapist. Strict adherence to dichotomies reinforces the inordinate amount of power ascribed to the therapist. Accompanying this power is the ongoing pressure on the therapist to fix or cure the problems in the client's life. Self-care and mutual respect are more likely cultivated within a collaborative relationship.

More attention needs to be given to the ways in which clients can teach therapists about their strengths, resources, and solutions that have been discovered in their past experiences. The counseling process can provide the therapist with the experience of vicarious healing and renewal. Being a witness to others' growth experiences reaffirms the belief in the capacity of individuals to function with a learned resourcefulness with respect to change, and the important role that counseling can play in cultivating this process.

Bibliography

Abney, V., Yang, J., and Paulson, M. (1992). Transference and counter transference issues unique to long-term group psychotherapy of adult women molested as children. *Journal of Interpersonal Violence, 7,* 559-569.

Adams-Westcott, J., Dafforn, T., and Sterne, P. (1993). Escaping victim life stories and co-constructing personal agency. In S. Gilligan and R. Price (Eds.). *Therapeutic conversations.* New York: W.W. Norton.

Anderson, L. and Gold, K. (1994). "I know what it means but it's not how I feel": The construction of survivor identity in feminist counselling practice. *Women & Therapy, 15,* 5-17.

Axelroth, E. (1991). Retrospective incest group therapy for university women. *Journal of College Student Psychotherapy, 5,* 81-100.

Bagley, C. and Ramsay, R. (1986). Sexual abuse in childhood: Psychosocial outcomes and implications for social work practice. *Journal of Social Work and human sexuality, 4,* 33-47.

Bass, E. and Davis, L. (1988). *The courage to heal: A guide for women survivors of child sexual abuse.* New York: Harper & Row.

Belenky, M., Clinchy, B., Goldberger, N., and Tarule, J. (1986). *Women's ways of knowing: The development of self, voice, and mind.* New York: Basic Books.

Bell-Gadsby, C. and Siegenberg, A. (1996). *Reclaiming herstory: Ericksonian solution-focused therapy for sexual abuse.* New York: Brunner/Mazel.

Boniello, M. (1990). Grieving sexual abuse: The therapist's process. *Clinical Social Work Journal, 18,* 367-379.

Briere, J. (1984). *The effects of childhood sexual abuse on later psychological functioning: Defining a "post-sexual-abuse syndrome."* Paper presented to the Third National Conference on Sexual Victimization of Children, Washington, DC.

Briere, J. (1988). The long-term clinical correlates of childhood sexual victimization. *Annals of the New York Academy of Science, 528,* 327-334.

Briere, J. (1989). *Therapy for adults molested as children: Beyond survival.* New York: Springer.

Briere, J. (1992). *Child abuse trauma: Theory and treatment of the lasting effects.* Newbury Park, CA: Sage.

Briere, J. and Runtz, M. (1987). Post sexual abuse trauma: Data and implications for clinical practice. *Journal of Interpersonal Violence, 2,* 367-379.

Briere, J. and Runtz, M. (1993). Childhood sexual abuse: Long-term sequelae and implications for psychological assessment. *Journal of Interpersonal Violence, 8,* 312-330.

Brigham, D. (1994). *Imagery for getting well: Clinical applications of behavioral medicine.* New York: W.W. Norton.

Browne, A. and Finkelhor, D. (1986). Impact of child sexual abuse: A review of the literature. *Psychological Bulletin, 99,* 66-77.

Butler, S. (1985). *Conspiracy of silence.* San Francisco, CA: Volcano Press.

Capacchione, L. (1991). *Recovery of your inner child.* New York: Simon and Schuster.

Carver, C., Stalker, C., Stewart, E., and Abraham, B. (1989). The impact of group therapy for adult survivors of childhood sexual abuse. *Canadian Journal of Psychiatry, 34,* November, 753-758.

Cohen, S. (1991). The art of loving. *New Women.* June, 79-82.

Combs, G. and Freedman, J. (1990). *Symbol, story and ceremony: Using metaphor in individual and family therapy.* New York: W.W. Norton.

Constable, D. (1994). The process of recovery for adult survivors of childhood sexual abuse: A grounded theory study. (Doctoral dissertation, University of Alberta, *Journal of Dissertation Abstracts International,* 56-02B.)

Conte, J. and Schuerman, J. (1987). Factors associated with an increased impact of child sexual abuse. *Child Abuse and Neglect, 11,* 201-211.

Courtois, C. (1988). *Healing the incest wound: Adult survivors in therapy.* New York: W.W. Norton.

Courtois, C. (1992). The memory retrieval process in incest survivor therapy. *Journal of Child Sexual Abuse, 1,* 15-31.

Crowder, A. (1995). *Opening the door: A treatment model for therapy with male survivors of sexual abuse.* New York: Brunner/Mazel.

Davis, L. (1990). *The courage to heal workbook: For women and men survivors of child sexual abuse.* New York: Harper & Row.

de Shazer, S. (1988). *Clues: Investigating solutions in brief therapy.* New York: W.W. Norton.

de Shazer, S. (1991). *Putting difference to work.* New York: W.W. Norton.

Dolan, Y. (1991). *Resolving sexual abuse: Solution-focused therapy and Ericksonian hypnosis for adult survivors.* New York: W.W. Norton.

Dolan, Y. (Revised 1993). Solution-focused recovery scale for survivors of sexual abuse. Original in Dolan, Y. (1991). *Resolving sexual abuse: Solution-focused therapy and Ericksonian hypnosis for adult survivors.* New York: W.W. Norton.

Evangeline, Judith. Absolution. Unpublished poetry. Used with permission.

Evangeline, Judith. I see myself. Unpublished poetry. Used with permission.

Evangeline, Judith. Striving for power song. Unpublished poetry. Used with permission.

Everson, M., Hunter, W., Runyon, D., Edelsohn, G., and Coulter, M. (1989). Maternal support following disclosure of incest. *American Journal of Orthopsychiatry, 59,* 197-207.

Faunce, P. (1990). The self-care and wellness of feminist therapists. In H. Lerman and N. Porter (Eds.), *Feminist ethics in psychotherapy* (pp. 185-194). New York: Springer.

Fedele, N. and Harrington, E. (1990). *Women's groups: How connections heal. Work in Progress,* No. 47. Wellesley, MA: Stone Center Working Paper Series.

Figley, C. (Ed.) (1995). *Compassion fatigue: Coping with secondary traumatic stress disorder.* New York: Brunner/Mazel.

Finkelhor, D. (1979). *Sexually victimized children.* New York: Free Press.

Finkelhor, D. (1987). The trauma of child sexual abuse: Two models. *Journal of Interpersonal Violence, 2,* 348-366.

Finkelhor, D. (1990). Early and long-term effects of child sexual abuse: An update. *Professional Psychology: Research and Practice, 25*(5), 325-330.

Finkelhor, D. and Browne, A. (1988). Assessing the long-term impact of child sexual abuse: A review and conceptualization. In L.E. Walker (Ed.), *Handbook on sexual abuse of children: Assessment and treatment issues* (pp. 55-71). New York: Springer.

Follette, V., Alexander, P., and Follette, W. (1991). Individual predictors of outcome in group treatment for incest survivors. *Journal of Consulting and Clinical Psychology, 59,* 150-155.

Follette, V., Polusny, M., and Milbeck, K. (1994). Mental health and law enforcement professionals: Trauma history, psychological symptoms, and impact of providing services to child sexual abuse survivors. *Professional Psychology: Research and Practice, 25,* 275-282.

Frank, F. and Treichler, P. (1989). Language, gender and professional writing: Theoretical approaches and guidelines for non-sexist usage. New York: MLA.

Friedrich, W. (1990). *Psychotherapy of sexually abused children and their families.* New York: W.W. Norton.

Funk & Wagnalls standard college dictionary. (1976). Toronto: Fitzhenry & Whiteside Limited.

Gannett, C. (1992). *Gender and the journal: Diaries and academic discourse.* New York State University of New York Press.

Ganzarain, R. and Buchele, B. (1986). Countertransference when incest is the problem. *International Journal of Group Psychotherapy, 36,* 549-566.

Geffner, R. (1992). Current issues and future directions in child sexual abuse. *Journal of Child Sexual Abuse, 1,* 1-13.

Gilgun, J. (1990). Factors mediating the effects of childhood maltreatment. In M. Hunter (Ed.), *The sexually abused male: Prevalence, impact, and treatment* (Vol. 1, pp. 177-190). Toronto: Lexington Books.

Gilligan, S. and Kennedy, C. (1989). Solutions and resolutions Ericksonian hypnotherapy with incest survivor groups. *Journal of Strategic and Systemic Therapies, 8,* 9-17.

Goulding, R. and Schwartz, R. (1995). *The mosaic mind: Empowering the tormented selves of child abuse survivors.* New York: W.W. Norton.

Grosch, W. and Olsen, D. (1994). *When helping starts to hurt: A new look at burnout among psychotherapists.* New York: W.W. Norton.

Hall, R., Tice, L., Beresford, T., Wooley, B., and Hall, A. (1989). Sexual abuse in patients with anorexia and bulimia. *Psychosomatics, 30,* 73-79.

Harter, S., Alexander, P., and Neimeyer, R. (1988). Long-term effects of incestuous child abuse in college women: Social adjustment, social cognition, and family characteristics. *Journal of Consulting and Clinical Psychology, 56,* 5-8.

Havens, R. and Walters, C. (1989). *Hypnotherapy scripts: A neo-Ericksonian approach to persuasive healing*. New York: Brunner/Mazel.

Havens, R. and Walters, C. (1993). *Hypnotherapy for health, harmony, and peak performance: Expanding the goals of psychotherapy*. New York: Brunner/Mazel.

Herman, J. (1992a). Complex PTSD: A syndrome in survivors of prolonged and repeated trauma. *Journal of Traumatic Stress, 5*, 377-391.

Herman, J. (1992b). *Trauma and recovery*. New York: Basic Books.

Higgins, G. (1994). *Resilient adults: Overcoming a cruel past*. San Francisco: Jossey-Bass.

Hyde, N. (1987). Uncovering the repression: Some clinical considerations in the psychotherapy of women incest survivors. *Alberta Psychology, 16*, 3-10.

Hyde, N. (1990). Voices from the silence: Use of imagery with incest survivors in T. A. Laidlaw and C. Malmo (Eds.), *Healing voices: Feminist approaches to therapy with women*. San Francisco: Jossey-Bass Publishers.

Jehu, D. (1989). *Beyond sexual abuse: Therapy with women who were childhood victims*. Chichester, UK: Wiley.

Johnson, L. (1995). *Psychotherapy in the age of accountability*. New York: W.W. Norton.

Jordan, J., Kaplan, A., Miller, J., Stiver, I., and Surrey, J. (1991). *Women's growth in connection: Writings from the Stone Center*. New York: Guilford Press.

Justice, B. and Justice, R. (1979). *The broken taboo*. New York: Human Sciences Press.

Kaplan, A., Gleason, N., and Klein, R. (1991). Women's self-development in late adolescence. In J. Jordon, A. Kaplan, J. Miller, I. Stiver, and J. Surrey (Eds,). *Women's growth in connection: Writings from the Stone Center* (pp. 122-131). New York: Guilford Press.

Katherine, A. (1991). *Boundaries: Where you end and I begin*. New York: Simon and Schuster.

Kirschner, S., Kirschner, D., and Rappaport, R. (1993). *Working with adult incest survivors: The healing journey*. New York: Brunner/Mazel.

Kottler, J. (1993). *On being a therapist*. San Francisco: Jossey-Bass.

Laidlaw, T. and Malmo, C., and Associates. (1990). *Healing voices: Feminist approaches to therapy with women*. San Francisco: Jossey-Bass.

Larson, N.R. and Maddock, J.W. (1984). Incest management and treatment: Family system vs. victim advocacy. Paper presented at the Annual Meeting of the American Association for Marriage and Family Therapy, San Francisco.

Lerner, H.G. (1985). *The dance of anger: A woman's guide to changing the patterns of intimate relationships*. New York: Harper & Row.

Lerner, H.G. (1989). *The dance of intimacy: A woman's guide to courageous acts of change in key relationships*. New York: Harper & Row.

Luthar, S. and Zigler, E. (1991). Vulnerability and competence: A review of research and resilience in childhood. *American Journal of Orthopsychiatry, 61*, 6-22.

Maltz, W. (1991). *The sexual healing journey: A guide for survivors of sexual abuse*. New York: Harper & Row.

Maltz, W. and Holman, B. (1987). *Incest and sexuality: A guide to understanding and healing.* Lexington, MS: Lexington Books.

Mason, M. (1991). *Making our lives our own: A women's guide to the six challenges of personal challenge.* San Francisco: Harper.

McBride, M. and Emerson, S. (1989). Group work with women who were molested as children. *Journal for Specialists in Group Work, 14,* 25-33.

McEvoy, M. (1990). Repairing personal boundaries: Group therapy with survivors of sexual abuse. In T. Laidlaw and C. Malmo (Eds.), *Healing voices: Feminist approaches to therapy with women.* San Francisco: Jossey-Bass.

McKay, M. and Fanning, P. (1992). *Self-esteem: A proven program of cognitive techniques for assessing, improving, and maintaining your self-esteem.* Oakland, CA: New Harbinger.

McLeod, W. (1986). *The Collins Paperback English Dictionary.* London: William Collins Sons & Co. Ltd.

Miller, J.B. (1991). Women and power. In J. Jordan, A. Kaplan, J.B. Miller, I. Stiver, and J. Surrey (Eds), *Women's growth in connection: Writings from the Stone Center.* New York: The Guilford Press.

Minns, K. M. (1982). Et cum spiritu tuo. In T. McNaran and Y. Morgan (Eds.), *Voices in the night: Women speaking about incest.* Minneapolis: Clais Press.

Moore, T. (1992). *Care of the soul: A guide for cultivating depth and sacredness in everyday life.* New York: Harper Collins.

Moore, T. (1996). *The re-enchantment of everyday life.* New York: Harper Collins.

Morrissey, K. (1982). *Self-help for women with a history of incest.* In *Therapeutic interventions in father-daughter incest.* Symposium conducted at the annual meeting of the American Psychological Association, Toronto, Ontario.

Morrow, S. and Smith, M. (1995). Constructions of survival and coping by women who have survived childhood sexual abuse. *Journal of Counseling Psychology, 42,* 24-33.

Napier, N. (1990). *Recreating your self: Help for adult children of dysfunctional families.* New York: W.W. Norton.

O'Hanlon, W.H. (1990). Debriefing myself: When a brief therapist does long-term work. *The Family Therapy Networker, 14*(2), 48-49, 68-69.

O'Hanlon, W. H. (1990). *The Family Therapy Networker, 14,* 48-49, 68-69.

O'Hanlon, W. H. and Martin, M. (1992). *Solution-oriented hypnosis: An Ericksonian approach.* New York: W.W. Norton.

Parks, A. and Goldberg, J. (1994). A current perspective on short-term groups for incest survivors. *Women & Therapy, 15,* 135-147.

Pearlman, L. and Mac Ian, P. (1995). Vicarious traumatization: An empirical study of the effects of trauma work on trauma therapists. *Professional Psychology: Research and Practice, 26,* 558-565.

Pearlman, L. and Saakvitne, K. (1995). *Trauma and the therapist: Countertransference and vicarious traumatization in psychotherapy with incest survivors.* New York: W.W. Norton.

Phillips, M. and Frederick, C. (1995). *Healing the divided self: Clinical and Ericksonian* hypnotherapy for post-traumatic and dissociative conditions. New York: W.W. Norton.

Porter, N. (1995). Therapist self-care: A proactive ethical approach. In E. Rave and C. Larsen (Eds.), *Ethical decision making in therapy: Feminist perspectives* (pp. 247-266). New York: The Guilford Press.

Rand, M. (in press). Self, boundaries and containment: An integrative body psychotherapy viewpoint. In C. Caldwell (Ed.). *Getting in touch: The guide to new body-centered therapies.* Wheaton, IL: Quest Books.

Rich, A. (1977). Conditions for work: The common world of women. In S. Ruddick and P. Daniels (Eds.), *Working it out* (pp. xiv-xxiv). New York: Pantheon.

Rich, A. (1979). *On lies, secrets, and silence: Selected prose—1966-78.* New York: W.W. Norton.

Root, M. and Fallon, P. (1988). The incidence of victimization experiences in a bulimic sample. *Journal of Interpersonal Violence, 3,* 161-173.

Rosenberg, J. and Rand, M. (1985). *Body, self & soul: Sustaining integration.* Atlanta, GA: Humanics.

Saakvitne, K. (1995). Therapists' responses to dissociative clients: Countertransference and vicarious traumatization. In L. Cohen, J. Berzoff, and M. Elin (Eds.), *Dissociative identity disorder: Theoretical and treatment controversies* (pp. 467-492). Northvale, NJ: Jason Aronson.

Satir, V. (1976). *Making contact.* Berkeley, CA: Celestial Arts.

Schauben, L. and Frazier, P. (1995). Vicarious trauma: The effects on female counselors of working with sexual violence survivors. *Psychology of Women Quarterly, 19,* 49-54.

Sedney, M. and Brooks, B. (1984). Brief communication: Factors associated with a history of childhood sexual experience in a nonclinical female population. *Journal of the American Academy of Child Psychiatry, 23,* 215-218.

Sgroi, S., Blick, L., and Porter, F. (1982). A conceptual framework for child sexual abuse. In S. Sgroi (Ed.), *Handbook of clinical intervention in child sexual abuse.* Lexington, MA: D.C. Heath.

Sprei, J. and Unger, P. (1986). *A training manual for the group treatment of adults molested as children.* Rockville, MD: Montgomery County Sexual Assault Service.

Stanley, L. and Wise, S. (1983). *Breaking out: Feminist consciousness and feminist* research. London: Routledge & Kegan Paul.

Steele, K. (1991). Sitting with the shattered soul. *Treating Sexual Abuse Today: The International Newsjournal of Abuse, Survivorship, and Therapy,* March/April, 12-15.

Steinem, G. (1992). *Revolution from within: A book of self-esteem.* Toronto: Little, Brown & Company.

Stinson, M. and Hendrick, S. (1992). Reported childhood sexual abuse in university counselling center clients. *Journal of Counselling Psychology, 39,* 370-374.

Trepper, T. (1986). The apology session. *Journal of Psychotherapy and the Family, 2,* 93-101.

Trepper, T. and Barrett, M. (1986). Vulnerability to incest: A framework for assessment. *Journal of Psychotherapy and the Family, 2,* 13-25.

Trepper, T. and Barrett, M. (1989). *Systemic treatment of incest: A therapeutic handbook.* New York: Brunner/Mazel.

Valentine, L. and Feinauer, L. (1993). Resilience factors associated with female survivors of childhood sexual abuse. *The American Journal of Family Therapy, 21,* 216-224.

van der Kolk, B. (1987). The role of group in the origin and resolution of the trauma response. In B. van der Kolk (Ed.), *Psychological trauma.* Washington, DC: American Psychiatric Press.

Wallas, L. (1985). *Stories for the third ear: Using hypnotic fables in psychotherapy.* New York: W.W. Norton.

Waller, G. (1992). Sexual abuse and bulimic symptoms in eating disorders: Do family interaction and self-esteem explain the links? *International Journal of Eating Disorders, 12,* 235-240.

Walters, C. and Havens, R. (1993). *Hypnotherapy for health, harmony, and peak performance: Expanding the goals of psychotherapy.* New York: Brunner/Mazel.

Weiser, J. (1993). *Phototherapy techniques: Exploring the secrets of personal snapshots and family albums.* San Francisco: Jossey-Bass.

Westurlund, E. (1992). *Women's sexuality after childhood incest.* New York: W.W. Norton.

White, M. (1993). Deconstruction and therapy. In S. Gilligan and R. Price (Eds.), *Therapeutic conversations.* New York: W.W. Norton.

White, M. and Epston, D. (1990). *Narrative means to therapeutic ends.* New York: W.W. Norton.

Wolin, S. and Wolin, S. (1993). *The resilient self: How survivors of troubled families rise above adversity.* New York: Villard Books.

Yassen, J. (1995). Preventing secondary traumatic stress disorder. In C. Figley (Ed.), *Compassion fatigue: Coping with secondary traumatic stress disorder in those who treat the traumatized.* New York: Brunner/Mazel.

Index

Page numbers followed by the letter "f indicate figures.